ADAPTED FOR YOUNG READERS

The
WOMAN'S
HOUR

ADAPTED FOR YOUNG READERS

The WOMAN'S HOUR

OUR FIGHT FOR THE RIGHT TO VOTE

ELAINE WEISS

RANDOM HOUSE NEW YORK

Photograph Credits: 1: New York State Library; 2: (top) New York Public Library,
(bottom) Library of Congress; 3: (both) Library of Congress;
4: (both) Tennessee State Library and Archives; 5: (both) Library of Congress;
6: (top) Calvin M. McClung Historical Collection, Knox County Public Library,
(bottom) Tennessee State Library and Archives; 7: (top) Library of Congress,
(bottom) Bryn Mawr College Special Collections; 8: Alan LeQuire

Visit us on the Web! rhcbooks.com

Educators and librarians, for a variety of teaching tools, visit us at
RHTeachersLibrarians.com

Library of Congress Cataloging-in-Publication Data
Names: Weiss, Elaine F., author. | Powell, Debbie, illustrator.
Title: The woman's hour : adapted for young readers / Elaine Weiss ;
illustrator, Debbie Powell.
Description: New York : Random House, [2020] | "The story of how America's women won
the right to vote, adapted for young adult readers" —Publisher. | Includes bibliographical
references and index. | Audience: Ages 8–12 | Audience: Grades 4–6
Identifiers: LCCN 2019053652 (print) | LCCN 2019053653 (ebook) |
ISBN 978-0-593-12518-2 (hardcover) | ISBN 978-0-593-12519-9 (library binding) |
ISBN 978-0-593-12520-5 (epub)
Subjects: LCSH: Women—Suffrage—Tennessee—History—20th century—Juvenile
literature. | Women—Suffrage—United States—History—20th century—Juvenile
literature. | Suffragists—Tennessee—History—20th century—Juvenile literature. |
Suffragists—United States—History—20th century—Juvenile literature. | United States.
Constitution. 19th Amendment—History—Juvenile literature.
Classification: LCC JK1911.T2 W45 2020 (print) | LCC JK1911.T2 (ebook) |
DDC 324.6/2309768—dc23

Printed in the United States of America
10 9 8 7 6 5 4 3 2 1
First Edition

For my children, Theodore and Abigail,
and the next generation of activists
working to improve our democracy

CONTENTS

INTRODUCTION

*I*magine if only half of the students in your school got to make all the decisions for everybody: what school clubs you could belong to, which sports teams were allowed to play, who could attend dances, who could write for the school newspaper. What if half of your friend group got to decide which kinds of things you could do—which parties you could attend, what clothes you were allowed to wear, what music you could listen to—while the other half just had to go along with those decisions?

What if only half of the *whole country* could have a say in how things worked, and made all the important decisions, while the other half could only watch?

Until 1920, that was the case in the United States of America. It wasn't until a century ago that women—half of the nation's population!—were given the right to have a voice in our government. In 1920, the Nineteenth Amendment to the U.S. Constitution gave American women the most important tool of democracy: the vote. Until then, men had been making decisions for the entire country. Only men had the right to vote. Only they could choose the nation's lawmakers and elected officials; only they could decide the laws and policies everyone had to follow. Women were excluded from making those choices.

The woman's suffrage movement changed all of that.

The suffrage movement was a long campaign to win the vote for women, but its goals went deeper than just achieving voting rights: it wanted to change society's attitudes about women.

Suffragist women weren't satisfied with being told they were less smart than men, less important, less capable. So they challenged those assumptions and worked to overturn traditional gender roles and the laws that upheld them.

Women and girls of all ages—daughters and mothers, friends and strangers—came together. They emboldened one another to speak out, to march in the streets, and to protest for the first time. Suffragists were willing to take serious risks to secure a better future for themselves and for generations to come.

It didn't happen overnight, and it wasn't easy. Winning the vote for women took seventy-two years of nonstop work. Three generations of dedicated, fearless suffragists— women and men, white and black—rolled up their sleeves to force change.

Through the decades, the fight to achieve woman's suffrage—"the Cause"—changed the way that society viewed women, and how women saw themselves. It unleashed a power and a potential that had *always* existed inside them but had previously been forced to stay hidden and quiet.

The women who campaigned for the vote faced anger and danger. They were criticized and insulted. They were pelted with rotten eggs and attacked on the street. Many were even imprisoned. Women of color in the suffrage movement faced additional problems: living in a segregated nation, they were too often kept at a distance by white suffragists.

Bravery and sisterhood motivated them all to keep fighting. They believed in a sense of justice, in democracy and equality. They believed in the intelligence and power of womankind. The suffrage movement developed talented women speakers and writers, organizers and politicians. And it opened up a world of possibility for the next generation of young women and girls.

Voting is a form of power, so this book is—as suffrage leader Alice Paul once described her main goal—about women and girls claiming their rightful powers. And it is also about the forces that fought intensely against them. Winning the vote was a breakthrough in American women's struggle for basic equality and respect. That struggle continues. It's up to us *all* to keep fighting.

And voting is just one way to do it. Even before turning eighteen and earning the right to vote, you have plenty of ways to get involved: join a campaign; write letters to your local and state representatives; become knowledgeable about a cause you care about. Stand up for equal rights for all Americans.

While reading about the events described in this book, you're going to encounter some disturbing language and attitudes. These expressions of racism and sexism were unfortunately commonplace in the United States a hundred years ago. Although they are, thankfully, less acceptable in today's society, the attitudes do persist. And our story's themes—power and politics, race and gender equality, citizenship rights and voting rights—remain urgent concerns. There is a heartening, even thrilling, lesson to be found here, too: ordinary women and girls banding together as activists, challenging an oppressive system, changing an entire country.

The summer of 1920, when the Nineteenth Amendment to the Constitution was coming close to approval by the states and woman's suffrage was on the verge of becoming national law, was a moment of reckoning for the entire country. Both sides—the suffragists and the antisuffragists—were determined to prevail. The outcome remained in doubt until the very last moment.

And it all began in July, with three women on their way to Nashville, Tennessee.

1 ★ THE CHIEF

*C*arrie Chapman Catt had spent the whole day sitting on a train, clattering over a thousand miles from New York City to Nashville, Tennessee. In the hours she wasn't reading field reports and legal documents, rimless eyeglasses perched on her nose, she was skimming the newspapers and sneaking in a few pages of a detective novel—she couldn't help it. Carrie loved a good mystery. She—the president of the National American Woman Suffrage Association (NAWSA), Susan B. Anthony's heir, the woman the suffragists called "the Chief"—had been called one last time to lead the fight to give women the vote. At least, she really *hoped* this would be the last time.

Her hair was silver and wavy now, but she had retained the sly smile, piercing blue eyes, and arched eyebrows that had always made her look either amused or annoyed depending on her mood. And she definitely wasn't amused this evening as her train rattled toward Tennessee in the dusky twilight of July 17, 1920. She was just plain worried.

Carrie's life's mission was to fight for freedom. American women still didn't have the most basic right of democracy: the vote. For more than seventy years—ever since the first women's rights meeting in Seneca Falls, New York, in 1848—generations of her suffrage sisters had faced public scorn as they campaigned, marched, and pleaded for their simple right to vote.

Now, finally, woman's suffrage was within sight.

The Tennessee legislature would be called into special session in a few weeks. Legislators—all men, of course—would gather to vote on ratifying the Nineteenth Amendment. If they ratified it, it would enter the U.S. Constitution and become the law of the land.

The Nineteenth Amendment was just one simple sentence, stating that a citizen's right to vote could not

A **legislature** is a group of lawmakers. Each state has its own legislature and its own state laws.

Legislators are lawmakers. They are the individuals who make up a **legislature**.

Legislatures meet, or are **in session**, at a specific time each year. A **special session** is when a legislature meets outside of its usual time frame.

To **ratify** an amendment is to pass it and make it officially U.S. law.

be denied on account of sex. Nothing revolutionary, according to Carrie Catt. It was only what she thought women—citizens of the United States—truly deserved.

A year earlier, in June 1919, the amendment had finally been pushed through both houses of the U.S. Congress after forty whole years of delay. Carrie had been overjoyed—and relieved—when *that* news arrived.

But passing through Congress was just the first step. The amendment then moved to the states for rati-

> The U.S. **Congress** makes laws for the entire United States of America. Congress is divided into two groups (known as **chambers**): the **House of Representatives** and the **Senate**. *Both* chambers must pass an amendment in order to ratify it.

fication. Carrie knew it would be a tough fight: suffragists had to convince at least thirty-six state legislatures to accept the amendment. By July 1920, thirty-five states had ratified the amendment. Nine had rejected it. Three were refusing to even consider it.

That left only Tennessee as a possible thirty-sixth state—the very last state needed to make American women's dreams of voting come true.

If the Suffs could only persuade the Tennessee legislature to pass the amendment, woman's suffrage would become American law. That meant every woman, in every state, would get to vote in every single election. That included local elections—like those for mayors, governors, and senators—as well as the election of the nation's president. It would spell victory at last—and just in time for the presidential election in a few months.

That is, assuming the suffragists could convince the state of Tennessee to support their cause.

Carrie's young assistant, Marjorie Shuler, had already arrived in Nashville to see what the Suffs were up against. Marjorie had met with the Tennessee suffrage leaders, talked to politicians, skimmed the newspapers, and eavesdropped on talk in the hotel lobbies. It hadn't taken her long to realize that Nashville was a hornet's nest. Word had it that the legislature was corrupt and that these politicians could be easily bribed. Plus, the governor, Albert Roberts, was caught in a nasty fight to hold on to his job and win his next election. Getting all tangled up with the amendment's ratification was the last thing he wanted to do.

Marjorie wasn't optimistic about the fight in Tennessee. She had sent a wire to NAWSA headquarters in New York that read, "Regard outlook hopeless under present conditions."

Carrie had bought her ticket to Nashville as soon as she received that message. For the past two weeks, she'd given her suffragist peers stern directions, warning them to get ready for an ugly fight: "The Anti-Suffs will flood Tennessee with the most outrageous literature it has ever been your lot to read," she told them, drawing from her experience in the other southern states. "It will contain outright lies, innuendoes, and near truths, which are more damaging than lies." Furthermore, she added, the race issue would be "put forth in the ways to arouse the greatest possible prejudice."

Carrie had been battling for woman's suffrage for so long. As her train sped past rural, tree-lined landscapes, she could still feel the sting of the very first time she had confronted injustice. Back then, she hadn't yet known women's rights was a "Cause" she could fight for.

Carrie grew up a pig-tailed Iowa farm girl, curious and a bit of a bookworm.

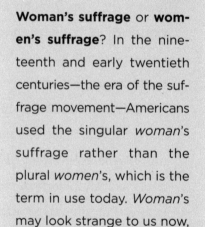

Woman's suffrage or **women's suffrage**? In the nineteenth and early twentieth centuries—the era of the suffrage movement—Americans used the singular *woman*'s suffrage rather than the plural *women*'s, which is the term in use today. *Woman*'s may look strange to us now, but it's historically accurate!

She often borrowed her father's newspapers, and she liked to chime in when her parents talked politics at the dinner table. Carrie's mother, especially, was well read and informed about so many important topics. Carrie wanted to be just like her.

But on Election Day 1872, with Ulysses Grant facing off against newspaper publisher Horace Greeley for the seat in the White House, thirteen-year-old Carrie had watched, confused, as her father prepared to ride into town to vote for the president while her mother remained home.

Shouldn't you be getting ready to go vote with the other grown-ups? Carrie had asked her mother. The whole family laughed. She still remembered the embarrassment, the hot tears welling up. Women weren't allowed to vote, her father explained, as if it were the most obvious thing in the world. Only men were allowed. Voting was much too important to be left to *women*!

Carrie was immediately angry: her mother knew as much about the candidates and the "important" issues as her father did, maybe even more! She deserved to vote for the president, too. And, worst of all, this meant that one day Carrie wouldn't be allowed to vote, either. Carrie didn't take kindly to rules that made it seem she was less important, less smart, or less capable than boys were. Those rules weren't *fair*.

So Carrie dedicated her life to changing the laws that barred women from voting. She became the famous leader of a giant army: nearly two million women and men were members of local NAWSA groups. Millions more were supporters of their movement. They all looked up to Mrs. Carrie Catt.

The train conductor called the next stop as Carrie flipped a newspaper open on her lap. She sighed as she read head-line after headline spelling bad news. The country was facing a number of problems, and the entire world was still strug-gling to rebuild two years after World War I

had ended. Seventeen million people had been killed in the war. And though many had hoped the end of the war would finally bring peace, Russia was invading Poland and advancing across Eastern Europe. Ottoman Turks were fighting the Greeks while continuing to massacre Armenians. Irish and British troops were fighting. Mexico was spiraling into civil war. A famine was spreading through China.

And on the home front, things were worse than before the war had begun! Underpaid steel mill, coal, railroad, and shipbuilding workers were striking all over the country. Acts of racism were increasing in many cities. Protests erupted in response. And throughout the whole country, the economy was faltering. People were having trouble making ends meet.

To top it all off, the U.S. Senate had recently rejected President Woodrow Wilson's plan to join the League of Nations to settle international disputes. Carrie thought the league was the only good thing to come out of the horrible war. It was an opportunity to bring countries together in the name of peace. Carrie believed in world peace as much as she believed in freedom. She'd written and spoken in favor of the League of Nations—the backlash against it disgusted her.

After World War I, the **League of Nations** was created to settle clashes between different countries and maintain world peace.

Despite all her hard work, Carrie knew that change only happened *really* slowly. She had hung a large "Suffrage Map" of the United States on the wall of her office. Different colors and patterns marked the types of suffrage available to women in each state. In some states, women were already able to vote in all elections; in others, they had "limited suffrage" and could vote only in certain types of elections, for school board or in other local elections. Colored in black on the map were the states where women couldn't vote at all. The federal amendment was the only way to change the election laws in every state at once—and change the entire map into an amazing, uniform design.

Carrie's train pulled into the station at about half past eight that Saturday evening. Reporters swarmed her as she made her way to the Hotel Hermitage. "Suffrage supporters feel certain that Tennessee will rise to the occasion and use its decisive vote for the women," Carrie told them confidently. "The eyes of the country and the world are centered here at Nashville." Carrie Catt was demonstrating the same brave, optimistic attitude that she encouraged the Tennessee Suffs to adopt—whether she believed it or not.

State governments make laws for their own states. As such, states make their own election laws. Federal laws (laws for the whole country) take precedence over state ones, though.

The federal government makes laws for the *whole* country—all fifty states. So a **federal amendment** applies to the entire United States.

Soot was flying in through the train's open windows, but Josephine Pearson had too much on her mind to care about dirtying her dress. She set her sharp eyes on the landscape ahead and tucked her wiry gray hair under her hat. Josephine couldn't get to Nashville soon enough. Earlier that day, she'd received a telegram alerting her that Carrie Catt was coming to Tennessee. "Our forces are being notified to rally at once. Send orders—and come immediately."

Josephine was the proud leader of the Tennessee Antis, formally known as the Tennessee State Association Opposed to Woman Suffrage. She was a professor and had been giving lectures and writing articles on the topic for years. The summons to Nashville thrilled her. This was the Antis' chance to destroy the woman's suffrage amendment, once and for all.

Josephine was fifty-two years old, and all her training—college, graduate degrees, and her years as a teacher—had prepared her for this mission. She knew she was following God's will. After all, the Bible said a woman's place was in the home as wife and mother. What was the point in disturbing the peace of a home by giving a woman the right to vote? Tennessee men knew what was best for their wives and daughters and would protect them. Josephine felt there was no need to question the wisdom of the men in charge, *or* the laws they had created. A woman's life was complicated enough, raising children, taking care of the home, supporting her husband—why add politics to the mix?

But Josephine wasn't just concerned with what the Bible said about women. Giving women the right to vote could destroy the white southern way of life, she feared.

After the Civil War and the mayhem of Reconstruction—
when black men had been granted the right to vote (and
some were even elected to
office)—the southern states
had finally, Josephine felt,
suppressed black people
with Jim Crow laws. But
if *all* women were allowed
to vote, that would have to
include black women, too.
Then Washington could de-
mand that black men be allowed to vote, and that was
totally unacceptable to her.

This would be Tennes-
see's time to triumph. And,
she prayed, Tennessee would
uphold its traditions. With

Jim Crow laws enforced racial segregation throughout
southern states until 1965.

After the Civil War, the
Fifteenth Amendment gave
black men the right to vote,
but restrictive Jim Crow
laws prevented black men
from voting in the south-
ern states. Voting rights for
black men and women in
the South were restored by
the Voting Rights
Act of 1965.

God's help, the Antis would hold fast against the feminist
epidemic sweeping the nation.

So, when the telegram had arrived late Saturday afternoon, it was with a sense of holy purpose and duty to the
traditions of southern culture that Josephine Pearson had
bought a one-way train ticket to Nashville.

The Hotel Hermitage in Nashville was a much grander

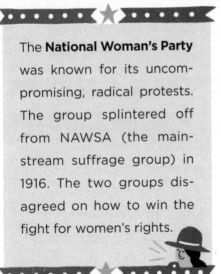

The **National Woman's Party** was known for its uncompromising, radical protests. The group splintered off from NAWSA (the mainstream suffrage group) in 1916. The two groups disagreed on how to win the fight for women's rights.

hotel than Josephine might normally have chosen for herself. When she checked in at the front desk, she requested the cheapest room and, she added, to please make sure it was as far away from Mrs. Carrie Catt as possible. After Josephine plunked down her suitcases and splashed cool water on her face, she took a deep breath and dialed her allies around the country to sound the alarm: *Mrs. Catt is here. Send help. We are under attack.*

On the same evening in mid-July, Sue Shelton White was heading to Nashville. She and Alice Paul, the head of the National Woman's Party, had been in Ohio before then. With banners and picket signs in hand, they had confronted the two men who wanted to be the next president of the United States: Governor James Cox was the surprise choice of the Democrats. The Republican candidate, Warren G. Harding, a senator from Ohio, was trying to play it safe with conservative policies. As her train approached the Nashville station, Sue White thought about each of the candidates. Both men seemed eager to please their constituents—but they were most likely unwilling to fight for the ratification of the Nineteenth Amendment. They would need to be convinced.

Sue White was by now, at age thirty-three, a veteran protester. Two years earlier, she'd left Carrie Catt's mainstream suffrage organization to join the more radical Woman's Party. Now Sue was one of Alice Paul's trusted deputies at the party's headquarters in Washington.

Constituents are the people whom a politician represents.

The Woman's Party was filled with ambitious young women who could no longer tolerate their second-class citizenship. And they were willing to put up a fight for it. Alice Paul was their quiet, ferocious, confident leader. Alice was a great risk-taker. She was always at the front line of every protest. She wasn't afraid of being arrested or threatened. As far as Alice could tell, the women of America had nothing to lose in the fight for freedom.

Sue White felt right at home in the radical Woman's Party. She didn't believe in behaving like a sweet southern lady, waiting around for men to give her rights. Quiet pleading and polite pleasantries didn't suit her. Sue was a rebel—a radical—and she was proud of it! She'd even been arrested at a suffrage protest and held in jail.

Sue looked the part of a modern career woman. She was stylish and her brunette hair was cut in a fashionable bob. Those who saw her in action called her "Lady Warrior." Everyone liked working with "Miss Sue," as she was affectionately called; they respected her intelligence, appreciated her sense of fairness, and enjoyed her sense of humor. She had an unfailingly sunny disposition and a warm smile, but she had no patience for the society set of Tennessee. Sue had grown up poor. She became an orphan at a young age, so she had always been responsible for taking care of herself. She made her own way, becoming a first-rate court reporter, and even started her own business. She wanted to study law, but the lawyers at the courthouse laughed at the idea of a woman lawyer. Still, Sue held on to the dream of becoming an attorney one day.

Now it was up to her to run the Woman's Party's campaign in Nashville, in her home state of Tennessee. She had already scoped out the situation—and it wasn't a pretty picture. Unless suffragists fought "relentlessly," she warned, Tennessee was in danger of being lost. And if they didn't win Tennessee, the amendment to give women the right to vote might never be passed! The suffragists' decades-long battle would be *over*.

Sue had never before been in charge of a state campaign by herself, and this was shaping up to be a campaign like no other. She was ready for the challenge.

2 ★ LAY OF THE LAND

*B*right sunshine beat down on Nashville the next morning. The city was Sunday quiet and groggy with heat. Stores on Church Street stood locked under rolled-up awnings. It was the Sabbath. But today was no day of rest for Carrie Catt. A busy afternoon lay ahead. Over a hundred of the city's most powerful people would be coming to meet her at her hotel room in the Hotel Hermitage.

In her third-floor room, Carrie clipped her pince-nez eyeglasses onto her lacy blouse. With her usual calm confidence, she took a deep breath and brushed aside the window curtain to peek onto the street. Sure, Nashville was going to be hard work, but she was never a woman to shrink from a challenge.

Even as a teenager, she'd refused to allow anyone to underestimate her abilities or stifle her ambitions. She'd yearned to go to college and study for a career like her brother would, but her father had tried to shoot down her dreams. Women didn't need so much education, he said, and anyhow, the family couldn't afford it.

That hadn't stopped Carrie. She'd found a job teaching and saved up enough money to put herself through Iowa Agricultural College, washing dishes and stamping library books to pay tuition. In school she'd been a trailblazer. She'd aced her classes and started a women's debate club. When she was excluded from "boys'" activities, she found ways to pursue those interests anyway, on her own terms. She didn't want to live in a world where men made all the rules. She wanted to create her own successes. Tall, dark-haired, and silver-tongued, she had set her sights high. She wanted to become a lawyer but couldn't afford law school on her own. So she worked many different jobs—everything from a newspaper editor to a high school principal—to save up for it.

Carrie also started working as a field organizer for the Iowa Woman Suffrage Association. Ever since that unforgettable morning in her family's kitchen, she'd felt passionately about a woman's right to vote. She just hadn't intended to

make a career of it—she didn't even realize that was an option. But once Carrie got involved in the suffrage association, there was no stopping her. It didn't take long for the older, more experienced suffragists to take notice. They quickly recognized her magnetic speaking skills, her innate ability to get a crowd excited about a common goal. Everyone could see that this Iowa girl had the fire to carry the Cause into the twentieth century.

In 1900, Susan B. Anthony had chosen Carrie to be the next president of the National American Woman Suffrage Association. That was twenty years ago, and here she was in Nashville, Tennessee, still fighting.

A knock at Carrie's hotel room door startled her for a second. She leapt up to greet Catherine Kenny.

Carrie had been looking forward to her conversation with Catherine. Catherine knew the lay of the Tennessee land like the back of her hand. It was she who'd organized the meet and greets for Carrie today. They had much to go over before their guests' arrival.

Catherine Kenny radiated optimism, but she never underestimated the challenges suffragists faced, especially in Tennessee. It took a whole lot of courage to be a Suff in her home state, she knew. It wasn't exactly considered a "respectable" calling. You had to grow a thick skin, and you had to learn to ignore (or laugh off) whatever people said about you. Catherine always made the suffrage movement seem enticing and fun, though, and her enthusiasm was contagious. Women who got to talking to her soon found themselves joining suffrage clubs.

Catherine was relieved that Carrie Catt—protégé of Susan B. Anthony herself!—had come all the way from New York to help Tennesseans. Really, they needed all the help they could get.

Catherine removed her hat and smoothed her dress before handing Carrie her reports. She'd gone over them herself that morning. The results of the first poll of the Tennessee legislature weren't exactly promising. Carrie studied them carefully. The suffragists had asked Tennessee delegates across the state whether they'd ratify the amendment for woman's suffrage. So far, only one-third of the men had responded positively. That wasn't much. Many delegates hadn't even bothered to reply. Some flat-out refused to ratify. Others said they'd support the amendment—they just weren't *quite* ready to be placed on the definite "Yes" list.

Catherine couldn't understand why these men were taking so long. This was urgent!

The previous year, Tennessee had passed a limited suffrage bill, giving women the vote in municipal and presidential elections.

Polls record which politicians, or which constituents, support which issues.

Women still had no say in choosing their congressmen or senators, but it was certainly better than nothing. Catherine had been so proud the day the bill was passed. Then she'd worked with Nashville's black suffragists to register black women and get out the vote. It made her proud to be a Tennessean. The women of Tennessee—and of the entire United States of America—were one step closer to *full* suffrage.

Carrie admired Catherine Kenny's political instincts and clever footwork, but the poll made her anxious. Not nearly enough legislators had agreed to support the Nineteenth Amendment, and there was no excuse for silencing the voices of *half the population*!

She wore a sunny smile to cloak her worry, though. It was always best to put on a strong front, Carrie thought.

Soon enough, a parade of visitors began knocking on her door, welcoming her to Tennessee. Dozens followed: district chairwomen of the new Tennessee League of Women Voters; Democratic Party ward chairmen; local politicians and newspaper editors who had bravely stood up for woman's suffrage for years. They all lined

The **Tennessee League of Women Voters** was founded in the spring of 1920, soon after Tennessee women were granted limited suffrage in 1919.

up to shake the hand of the Chief. Tennessee could do it, they said. It could really be the thirty-sixth state! If only she would lead them.

The stream of guests continued as the sun slid down in the darkening blue sky.

It was one thing to talk to these friends of suffrage, Carrie thought as the last visitor waved good-bye. Now on to its foes.

Josephine Pearson was reading through a stack of telegrams that Sunday morning when the phone rang. Her friend Queenie Washington had arrived at the Hotel Hermitage to greet her, with a crew of Tennessee Antis in tow. Josephine couldn't wait to be reunited with them.

On the seventh floor of the Hermitage, she and Queenie got down to business writing to-do lists and handing out tasks to their peers. They started planning rallies, dinner parties, and teas. Anything to get the anti-ratification word out there.

Josephine had been the president of the Tennessee State Association Opposed to Woman Suffrage since 1917, leading her fellow Antis in the fight *against* gender equality. The prominent lawyer John Vertrees had offered her the job. Vertrees—the man she considered her mentor—was a member of the American Constitutional League, the men's wing of the Antis. His 1916 manifesto, *To the Men of Tennessee on Female Suffrage*, made his hostility to woman's suffrage crystal clear.

Women were irrational and less intellectual than men, John Vertrees argued. They were too emotional to vote on policy matters, anyway. And besides, he added, their physical weaknesses, like pregnancy and periods, made them totally unfit for office.

John Vertrees's manifesto also included a twist: if women could vote, they would be torn from their role as homemakers and plunged into the dirty world of politics—the whole order of southern society would be destroyed! Furthermore, equal suffrage would place black women on the same level as white women, and that was not acceptable. John Vertrees was convinced that African Americans were inferior purely based on the color of their skin. The idea of racial equality disgusted him.

The South's social order had already been torn apart fifty years ago, first by the Civil War, then by Reconstruction. The ghosts of the war still haunted the southern states.

Then, a year ago, in 1919, the suffragists had pressed for limited suffrage rights. The legislature had eventually given in to their demands. It had been a humiliating defeat for the Antis. Women—both white and black—had been at the polls during last fall's elections. No way were the Antis going to let that happen again.

Josephine agreed with John Vertrees on all counts. She wanted to do him proud. And now every Anti woman in Tennessee was going to spread the message: woman's suffrage wasn't welcome in their state. Charlotte Rowe, the Antis' fiercest spokeswoman, was already on her way to Nashville from Anti headquarters in New York City. Two former-suffragists-turned-Antis, Kate Gordon and Laura Clay, were bringing their inside knowledge of Carrie Catt and those NAWSA Suffs. They'd already been so helpful in putting a stop to ratification throughout the South.

World War I had changed things for women, and not for the better, Josephine was convinced. While men were off fighting, women had taken up men's work. They'd gone off to the coal mines, to the fields, and into the streetcars. They'd even donned men's clothes.

The worst part of it was—these "modern women" actually *liked* it! Some of them wanted to stay put at their new jobs, even after the men had returned from war. Josephine couldn't understand it. How could these women choose to drive a truck, or toil away in a factory or an office? How could they think they were strong enough to labor like men? Being homemakers, raising children, and giving men support: *those* were their God-given duties. Anything else was simply unladylike. Feminism was going to destroy civilization, Josephine just knew it.

Take these suffragists right here in Nashville. They were scandalous! Especially those young ones in short skirts, their legs bare, their corsets thrown away, their hair short and boyish. It was disgusting! It was dangerous. It frightened her.

And that Carrie Catt was the very worst of them, Josephine and Queenie agreed with a sneer. Mrs. Catt was the symbol of all that was evil, ungodly, and un-American: a vile, feminist Yankee.

3 ⋆ TO EACH HER OWN

*A*s Nashville buzzed with energy on Sunday afternoon, Sue White took a quiet moment in her hotel room. She needed to focus. Carefully, she unfolded a large map of Tennessee. The state's rugged beauty—its soaring mountains, its plunging valleys, its flowing rivers and creeks—was going to make things very difficult for the Woman's Party.

That's because Sue and her women were going to have to travel up and down the whole length of Tennessee. Ninety-seven different counties—and some of them couldn't even be reached by train. There were 132 legislators, and the Woman's Party had to reach every single one of them.

Sue bit her lip. She knew it wouldn't be easy. But ever since she was a little girl, she'd been used to hardscrabble.

After all, she was orphaned at a young age and had to learn early on what it meant to work for her own food and shelter. She never let herself get stuck in the past or daydream about what she was missing. She only knew how to move forward. Being independent and working hard was in her bones. No matter how challenging it would be to find these legislators, Sue and her colleagues would do it.

Sue's suffrage journey had started with Carrie Catt's group, NAWSA. Back when America entered the First World War in April 1917, she'd believed that helping with the war effort would show men—once and for all—that women were valuable citizens. That they *deserved* the vote. But still male politicians would hardly budge on the issue of suffrage. And Sue grew impatient with NAWSA's cooperation with President Woodrow Wilson and other politicians. As far as Sue could tell, these men were barely lifting a finger to support women's rights. She and her fellow Suffs were just as smart and informed as the men were. Sue was sick of waiting around.

That was before she'd even really heard of Alice Paul and her radical Woman's Party. Alice Paul had refused to support America's involvement in the war in Europe. She and her troops picketed the White House, marching with banners that mocked the president. How could America send its sons to die for democracy in Europe, Alice demanded, while denying women the number one right of democracy—the vote—at home?

Lobbying means trying to convince politicians to support certain issues.

Both NAWSA and the Woman's Party set their sights on the same goal— suffrage—but they pursued it in their own ways. Each group did its own polling, lobbying, and organizing. The more Sue learned about the Woman's Party, the more she realized *it* was her style. NAWSA Suffs had manners and grace, sure. But they compromised too much for Sue's taste. Alice Paul and her radical, protesting ladies may have been loud, combative, and not a bit ladylike. They may have been called uncooperative, unpatriotic, and even traitors. But Sue saw them as freedom fighters. And that's just what drew her to them.

Sue knew what needed to be done in order for Tennessee to ratify. After all, she'd lived there her entire life. After years of working in the state's courthouses as a reporter, she'd met plenty of important political players. She knew their backgrounds, their allies, their soft spots. She could talk to anyone, Democrat or Republican. She wasn't easily intimidated.

It was time to show these Tennessee men—from senators and congressmen to Governor Albert Roberts himself—that suffrage was long overdue.

In the Governor's Mansion, Albert Roberts groaned to himself. He was short, with a small paunch, big ears, and bushy brows. He punched his arm into a rumpled jacket sleeve and wrapped a too-short tie around his neck. The day ahead was full of meetings. He had enough on his plate, worrying about his upcoming election. Winning a second term as governor was his greatest concern. The pesky issue of amendment ratification was the very last thing he wanted to think about.

Tennessee had enough problems already. Unions were striking throughout the state, from shoe manufacturers to railway workers, demanding fair pay. Albert had tried to clamp down on them quickly with police force—he couldn't have anyone thinking the governor was a weakling. Meanwhile, thousands of people had been out of work since the end of the war. And the Ku Klux Klan was appearing more and more throughout the state, assaulting and murdering black people.

Not to mention that Tennessee had some of the lowest literacy rates in the country. Albert wanted to change that. Kids should be going to school past the eighth grade, he believed. Teachers should be getting better training. Not everyone was on board with that, though. Manufacturers thought children should be working in factories, not "wasting time" in school.

Albert wanted Tennessee to thrive. He thought the state should be a leader in the South. It needed better education and better roads, all paid for by fairer taxes. Sure, everyone nodded in agreement, but no one wanted to pay.

On top of all this came the Nineteenth Amendment to give women the right to vote. Albert really wasn't sure what to do about it. He was being pressured by all sides. On one hand, the Tennessee suffragists demanded he call a special session of the legislature and ratify quickly. Even President Woodrow Wilson, his hero, was urging him to do it.

On the other hand, Albert's advisers warned him not to support suffrage. The Antis were some of his greatest friends and supporters—and they were rich, too. That meant they could contribute money to his campaign, which could potentially help him win the election.

Albert's advisers also reminded him that if women got the vote, they might not even vote *for* him. Those Suffs would no doubt remember he'd started his career as an Anti.

There was another knotty reason to be wary of giving women a political voice: many of the big corporations in the state didn't like the idea one bit. The Louisville and Nashville Railroad, known as the L&N, was dead set against women voting. The L&N had started bribing the Tennessee legislators long ago, giving them free tickets and high-paying jobs on the side in exchange for looking out for railroad interests and regulations. Unpredictable women voters could easily destroy this secret trade-off between men.

And what about the whiskey industry? If women were allowed to vote, they might want to *really* enforce Prohibition laws, which could once and for all ban liquor across the country. The state's cotton cloth mills and clothing makers were also strictly Anti. Women would probably vote for labor reform, or call for equal pay, or, worse yet, demand the end of child labor. The entire cotton-manufacturing economy of the South was run on the cheap labor of women and children. Was Governor Roberts willing to destroy all of that, just for the promise of a few women's votes?

And don't forget, Albert's advisers warned: black women

who would also be going to the polls would vote Republican, the party of Lincoln!

Yes, Albert grumbled, straightening his tie as he headed to his first meeting, these suffragists were causing him nothing but headaches.

4 ★ SENECA FALLS, 1848

*T*he early advocates of woman's suffrage all began their activist careers as abolitionists in the American Anti-Slavery Society. Lucretia Mott, Susan B. Anthony, and Elizabeth Cady Stanton worked together with Frederick Douglass to win the freedom of enslaved Americans and secure the rights of women. They helped grow two historic movements.

Elizabeth Cady Stanton was the bright, courageous daughter of a wealthy New York family. As a young woman, she traded the cliquey, elite social world around her for the rough-and-tumble of activism. It was her cousin Gerrit Smith who lured her in. Gerrit was a fierce abolitionist. His country manor hosted radicals and fugitive slaves (it was even a station on the

Abolitionists were antislavery activists who fought for the freedom of enslaved people.

Underground Railroad). Elizabeth spent many visits there as she grew up, listening to debates on politics and religion.

She recalled that once, as a little girl, in a fit of rage, she had decided it was up to her to destroy the laws that oppressed women. So she planned to take a pair of scissors and snip all the sexist laws out of her father's law books. When her dad got wind of her silly plan, he explained that a pair of scissors was not an effective way to change the law; when she grew up, she would have to convince Congress and state legislatures to change the discriminatory laws.

So that's just what Elizabeth did. She joined forces with like-minded men and women in the American Anti-Slavery Society and then the suffrage movement, fighting for equality. The American abolitionist leaders William Lloyd Garrison and Wendell Phillips had always insisted on gender equality in the American Anti-Slavery Society. Women in the group had just as much say as the men. Together they organized, raised money, and spoke freely in debates. But outside of their feminist-leaning group was a different story. Women were excluded from other abolitionist meetings and debates.

It made Lucretia and Elizabeth furious. How could abolitionist men promote freedom but not even allow women to speak in their meetings? The nerve! One day, the women decided, they'd gather their *own* meeting. A meeting specifically dedicated to demanding equality for women.

Elizabeth was by then married to Henry Brewster Stanton, a progressive abolitionist. They lived a quiet life in Seneca Falls, a small town in the Finger Lakes district of New York. Housework was a bore to Elizabeth—but it was the perfect time to dream of rebellion.

In 1848, she, Lucretia, and three other friends decided to finally do it: to call that meeting about women's rights. The Woman's Rights Convention would be held at the Methodist Wesleyan Chapel in Seneca Falls.

Elizabeth made a list of the women's main principles. Modeled after the Declaration of Independence, this Declaration of Sentiments pointed out the "different code of morals for men and women." It demanded women receive equal pay for equal work. It raised issues ranging from divorce and giving mothers custody rights of their children to allowing women to own property. And it declared that women and girls should have the right to attend college, to have professions and interests of their *own*.

But there was one issue Elizabeth listed that was considered the most controversial: the right to vote. Women couldn't have any *real* power until they had a say in politics, Elizabeth felt. She'd talked about the issue a lot with her friend Frederick Douglass. Frederick Douglass had escaped slavery just a decade before. In that time, he'd made a name for himself as an activist, writer, and publisher of an abolitionist newspaper. And he was an unabashed "Woman's Rights Man." Slaves, free blacks, and women were—to varying degrees—all shackled by American laws, Frederick said. And so it was time to change them. Elizabeth couldn't have agreed more. She was thrilled that Frederick would travel to Seneca Falls for the convention.

The scene outside the Wesleyan Chapel was bursting with energy. Hundreds of women and men arrived on horseback and on foot—far more people than the suffragists had ever dreamed would attend. The chapel was packed. A hushed awe swept the crowd as the passionate talks and debates began.

The meeting stretched over two days, from mornings till late nights. On the second day, Elizabeth Cady Stanton stood to read aloud the Declaration of Sentiments. Her proud voice rang through the chapel. The crowd was electrified, nodding and murmuring admiringly at each of her points. Until she declared the need for woman's suffrage, that is. Gasps arose throughout the chapel.

Frederick Douglass stepped forward then, ready to defend his friend. The vote, he agreed, addressing the crowded chapel, was the only way for women and black people to be heard. It was the key to freedom. Yes, it was a big step, but now was the time to be bold.

Word of the Seneca Falls meeting spread. Newspapers condemned it with angry headlines. Journalists mocked it in opinion pieces. Ministers delivered scolding sermons, warning of the suffragists' sinfulness.

Elizabeth Cady Stanton couldn't help but laugh as she flipped through the newspapers in the following days and weeks. "That is just what I wanted," she gleefully wrote to Lucretia Mott. "It will start women thinking, and men too; and when men and women think about a new question, the first step in progress is taken."

By 1850, the women's rights crusade was growing. Activists like William Lloyd Garrison, Frederick Douglass, Sarah and Angelina Grimké, and Sojourner Truth all joined the Cause.

The next year, Elizabeth met a thirty-year-old teacher turned Anti-Slavery Society organizer named Susan Anthony. Susan was tall, proper, and always disciplined when it came to her work. The chatty and mischievous Elizabeth instantly clicked with her. On the outside, they might have seemed like opposites, but their personalities balanced each other out perfectly. They became close friends and collaborators. "I forged the thunderbolts, and she hurled them," was the way Elizabeth described her political partnership with Susan.

In May 1863, Elizabeth and Susan started an activist group called the Women's National Loyal League. It proudly mixed feminist and abolitionist views. "There can never be true peace in this republic until the civil and political rights of all citizens of African descent and all Women are practically established," the league asserted.

Their plan was clear: to push President Abraham Lincoln to abolish slavery forever. So they recruited thousands of women to go door-to-door, collecting the signatures of women and men, white and black, demanding an end to slavery.

Senator Charles Sumner of Massachusetts, an ardent abolitionist, presented these petitions to Congress. It's no coincidence that a constitutional amendment abolishing slavery soon passed. The work of these women activists is credited with helping to convince Lincoln and Congress to push through the Thirteenth Amendment.

Elizabeth and Susan had just built the very first national women's political organization in the United States. And they had seen firsthand the power of women in action.

★ ★ ★

After the Civil War, the United States Congress passed the Fourteenth and Fifteenth Amendments to give black men the rights of citizens and the right to vote. But the amendments left women—of all races—out.

Susan and Elizabeth were furious. Frederick Douglass was also upset that the laws would not include women. But as he pointed out to Susan and Elizabeth, life in America for black men—who had been enslaved, who were being lynched and attacked regularly—was significantly more dangerous than for white women like themselves. In order to help protect his fellow black men, Frederick had to make an excruciating choice, against his wishes, to support amendments that excluded women.

Some suffragists agreed with Frederick Douglass. But Susan and Elizabeth were still outraged and even fought *against* the Fourteenth and Fifteenth Amendments because the laws didn't include voting rights for women. Nonetheless, Douglass continued to fight for woman's suffrage and remained friends with Susan and Elizabeth until his death.

In 1869, Susan and Elizabeth formed the National Woman Suffrage Association (the very group that Carrie Catt would eventually lead). Though they tried other strategies first, they eventually decided their goal was to add a woman's suffrage amendment to the United States

Constitution. Their proposed amendment boiled it down to one simple sentence, leaving no room for confusion: "The right of citizens of the United States to vote shall not be denied or abridged by the United States or by any State on account of sex."

Senator Aaron Augustus Sargent of California, a friend of the Suffs, introduced the amendment into the Senate on January 10, 1878. The lawmakers could barely contain their laughter. Votes—for *women*? *Dream on,* the men chuckled, shaking their heads in disbelief.

That one sentence-long amendment sat in Congress for the next forty years—every time it was brought up for a vote, it wouldn't pass. Lawmakers wouldn't touch it. It would ruin their careers, they reasoned.

During those forty long years, the suffrage movement grew and spread across the whole country. And it changed hands, too. Susan Anthony passed the NAWSA torch on to Carrie Catt. Women who'd been little girls when the movement first started were now suffrage warriors.

It wasn't until January 1918 that the U.S. House of Representatives *finally* passed the amendment. Over a year later, in June 1919, the Senate followed. It squeaked through with a margin of votes you could count on one hand.

When Carrie Catt heard that news, she broke into a wild

dance, stomping all over the house, whooping and singing. But she knew this was only the first step. There was still hard work to be done.

Next, the amendment would go on to the states. Thirty-six states had to ratify it. The first votes rolled in effortlessly. Illinois, Wisconsin, and Michigan. New York whisked ratification through in less than three hours.

Within the first three months, seventeen states ratified the amendment. Then the trouble began. More and more states were rejecting the amendment.

Both NAWSA and the Woman's Party headquarters had sent their women on the road to get the word out, get people excited about ratification. Marjorie Shuler and Sue White had both hit the trails, giving talks and meeting with other activists across the country. Carrie herself had jumped on a train on a tour of western states—she gave pep talks and negotiated with politicians. She encountered women she'd worked with in her very first campaigns, in the horse-and-buggy days. The women were old and stooped but still fighting, and they traveled far to see Carrie again.

Still, by the end of 1919 only twenty-two states had ratified. It wasn't until spring 1920 that the thirty-fifth state ratified. The Suffs needed thirty-six. But since March, nothing had moved forward. The governors of Connecticut,

Vermont, and Florida refused to call special sessions to consider the amendment. They wouldn't budge.

And now Tennessee was the suffragists' very last chance to secure a thirty-sixth state and make their dreams of voting in the 1920 elections come true. Victory was so close, they could taste it.

Everything was riding on this moment in Nashville.

5 ★ THE CANDIDATES

*P*resident Woodrow Wilson awoke from another nightmare. In his bedroom, in the private quarters of the White House, his butler, Brooks, and his wife, Edith, entered quickly. His morning guests would be here soon, they reminded him urgently. Brooks helped him to dress, pulling a starched white shirt over his listless left arm. Then Edith draped a shawl over her husband's left side. She didn't want their visitors to be able to see that Woodrow was partially paralyzed. She thought it wasn't anyone's business that he had had a stroke.

Several blocks away, Democratic presidential and vice presidential nominees James Cox and Franklin Roosevelt tied Windsor knots onto their collars. They wanted to look their best when they went to see President Wilson at the White House on this fine July morning.

A few weeks earlier, they had won the Democratic nomination at the party convention (there were no primary elections for party picks at that time). President Wilson's blessing would mean a lot to Cox and Roosevelt. They were planning to be the future of the Democratic Party.

Woodrow Wilson wasn't at all sure he *wanted* to give that blessing. Wilson's own presidency had been full of conflict and controversy. There was the war, of course. That deadly, tragic, costly war. Then there was his mission of trying—and failing—to sell the Treaty of Versailles and the League of Nations to the American people. Wilson had wanted to build a foundation for lasting peace. He felt he must prevent the world from sliding into war yet again. The League of Nations was the way to do it. President Woodrow Wilson had a feeling that women would vote for the league—and that's why he had decided to support woman's suffrage. But that hadn't always been the case.

President Woodrow Wilson hadn't exactly been a fan of the women's movement. A Presbyterian minister's son with a conservative upbringing, he'd always tried to avoid the issue of woman's suffrage. Women were meant to be at home, he thought. Not voting. Not having opinions about important things, like politics. That was the job of men.

When Wilson became president, Alice Paul and the Woman's Party decided there was just one way to get him to take woman's suffrage seriously. They were going to wave the issue right under his nose until he couldn't ignore it any longer. So, on March 3, 1913, the day before Wilson's inauguration, Alice organized a huge suffrage parade through Washington. More than five thousand marchers—including Carrie Catt—paraded down Pennsylvania Avenue, banners in hand.

Wilson could still remember that protest. Washington had never seen anything like it. Women marching? Demanding rights? Mobs of men approached the parade and threw women to the ground, pulling their banners from their hands and smashing them to bits. Women were bruised and pushed, their clothes ripped. The police stood by and watched—they did not even try to protect the women.

The march, and the violent backlash, made front-page headlines.

It was bad press for the president. Women making a fuss. Violence and protests in front of the White House. And all the day before his inauguration.

Within the next months, Suffs bombarded Wilson. They demanded that women be given a voice in the United States of America. Still, Wilson squirmed and avoided them. Finally, in October 1915, when he was facing reelection, he announced his support for woman's suffrage—but only if granted by the states, not by federal amendment.

His reasoning was strictly political. Wilson wanted to win back progressive voters who were against some of his first-term policies, which included getting involved in the war, restricting free speech, and segregating the federal workforce. He also wanted to win the support of women in western states who already could vote. If he didn't throw support behind suffrage now, there was no *way* they'd vote for him.

Alice Paul hadn't been impressed with Wilson's about-face on suffrage. Carrie Catt saw a potential ally in him, though. Carrie had been strictly against the war. Still, after the United States entered the European conflict in the spring of 1917, she sensed that throwing her support behind the League of Nations and bringing the women of America to President Wilson's side would be rewarded in the long run. So, temporarily, NAWSA prioritized war work, though they still kept up their demands for the vote.

Wilson was grateful for her help. From that time on, the president always listened to Carrie Catt and considered her requests.

Between Carrie's wartime cooperation and Alice Paul's loud protestation, both women could take credit for showing President Wilson that American democracy should begin at home: women deserved to vote. And now, after the war, Wilson needed women to support his plan for the League of Nations. It wasn't nearly as popular with men as he'd hoped it would be.

Democratic presidential candidate James Cox had dashed to Washington to meet President Wilson directly from a meeting with the Woman's Party. Alice Paul and Sue White really were spark plugs, he thought. And stubborn, too. They wouldn't take no for an answer.

"My time, my strength, and my influence will be dedicated to your cause," he'd told the women. He promised to do "everything in [his] power" to see the federal amendment through and make women's political rights the law of the land.

Cox knew very well that the upcoming ratification vote in Tennessee was a chance to give the Democratic Party a boost. He would try his best to nudge Governor Albert Roberts to pass the amendment in Tennessee. Get all those women on board for November, thankful to Democrats. Then they'd vote for *him* in the presidential election. Without women's votes, he wasn't quite sure he'd have enough to win the upcoming election.

Franklin Delano Roosevelt, a brash young assistant secretary of the navy, was Cox's running mate. Roosevelt was an appealing candidate. He had a famous name, Ivy League connections, and good looks and charm. Democrats also hoped he would appeal to suffragists, who counted FDR as a dependable, longtime friend of the Cause.

Cox hoped they had the White House in the bag.

In Marion, Ohio, just a few states west of James Cox and President Wilson's meeting in Washington, D.C., Warren Gamaliel Harding was rehearsing a speech. Harding liked to think of himself as a likable guy. Whether he was *respected* was another story. He was a bit of a follower. Usually he just watched where the political winds blew and sailed with them.

Today, Warren G. Harding wanted to captivate his audience like he never had before. This balmy July afternoon was the official start of his campaign to be the next Republican president of the United States.

Marion, Ohio, had never experienced anything quite like it. Republican legislators and thousands of spectators poured in. Every store downtown was dressed up in red, white, and blue bunting. Every house had a photo of Harding in its front window.

At two o'clock that afternoon, Harding greeted his audience at Marion's Chautauqua pavilion. The crowd of thousands stood on their chairs, cheering wildly and waving flags as he took the stage.

If you'd squinted closely at the crowd, though, you might have caught sight of a small group of women who *weren't* cheering. They were members of the Woman's Party. They'd come to scope out this presidential candidate; to see where he stood on woman's suffrage.

Harding's speech that afternoon urged a "return to normalcy" after the war. It was time to put "America first," he said—meaning to *avoid* Woodrow Wilson's League of Nations. Harding was a conservative. He didn't want to make changes to America's social order. The way things were— with America looking out for itself, and white men holding most of the power—was just fine by him.

The Woman's Party members listened to his speech and

tapped their toes impatiently. Finally, toward the end of Harding's speech, he nodded to the topic they wanted to hear about: woman's suffrage.

"The womanhood of America . . . is about to be enfranchised," Harding said. "It is my earnest hope, my sincere desire, that the one needed State vote be quickly recorded in the affirmative of the right of equal suffrage and that the vote of every citizen shall be cast and counted in the approaching election."

The Woman's Party members' ears perked up. It wasn't exactly a ringing endorsement, but it was at least *something*.

Then, always eager to please, Harding tried to soothe the worries of the nation's Antis as well: "And to the great number of noble women who have opposed [woman's suffrage], I venture to plead that they will accept the full responsibility of enlarged citizenship and give . . . their suffrage and support."

The Suffs rolled their eyes and groaned. Harding was so wishy-washy.

From Washington, Alice Paul made her annoyance with Harding's lukewarm support clear to reporters: "Only by action and not by the expression of polite interest will women be satisfied."

6 ★ THE MIRE OF POLITICS

The Nashville Antis wasted no time and launched their fight against ratification in Tennessee in July.

First, the American Constitutional League, the men's Anti group, started sending threatening letters to Governor Albert Roberts. If he knew what was good for his career, they said, he'd better drop the amendment.

Presidential nominee James Cox received an even sharper note from Nina Pinckard, president general of the Southern Women's Rejection League.

Who did he think he was, meeting with all these "militant" Woman's Party suffragists? she demanded furiously. Southern Antis wouldn't stand for it! "The very safety of Southern civilization, the purity of Anglo-Saxon blood, is involved in this Amendment," Mrs. Pinckard noted, displaying the racist attitudes rampant among some of her southern Anti peers. And anyhow, she added, as an Ohio politician, what happened in Tennessee was *none* of his business.

The Antis also turned their fire on Senator Warren G. Harding. All they'd asked of him was that he *not* poke his nose into Tennessee. But recently he'd begun talking about his "earnest hope" and "sincere desire" for ratification. The Antis demanded he explain such double-talk. They were just as annoyed as the Suffs were by Harding's desire to please both Antis and Suffs. Whose side was he on, anyway?

Charlotte Rowe, field secretary of the National Association Opposed to Woman Suffrage, swept into Tennessee's Union Station in a whites-only train car during that third week of July. As usual, she was very fashionably dressed, with a knot of auburn hair tied low on her neck, a broad-brimmed hat framing her face. She was a New Yorker in her late thirties with a quick wit, a sharp mind, and an even sharper tongue. She spoke her mind freely and eloquently, and she could cut to ribbons anyone who disagreed with her.

Like Carrie Catt, Charlotte was something of a celebrity. Reporters followed her as she walked briskly from the station to the Hotel Hermitage.

"We are determined to prevent women from descending to the political level of men," she said coolly, responding to their questions on ratification, "which if accomplished, will cheapen women and draw them into the mire of politics."

Charlotte herself was an experienced political figure who was already deep in the very "mire" she believed women should avoid. She was hands down the Antis' fiercest speaker. The Suffs absolutely couldn't stand her. They also couldn't help grudgingly admiring her, just a bit. If her opinions hadn't been so terrible, they thought, she might have been a great advocate for the Cause. Mostly the suffragists refused to debate her. They simply ignored her. Which was a shame for Charlotte; what she loved best was tangling with the veteran Suffs. She was always ready for a showdown.

Josephine Pearson greeted Charlotte's arrival at the Hotel Hermitage with gracious southern hospitality. Being in the company of such important women as Charlotte Rowe and Nina Pinckard made Josephine almost giddy with delight. This time around, it would be women leading the fight for the Antis. Not just men. Until now, no Tennessee

Anti woman had set foot in the statehouse to lobby legislators to support their cause.

This time they were going to be out in front.

The Antis came from many backgrounds, but they were united in one belief: keeping "traditional" gender roles in place. They feared the changes that equal suffrage would bring. Because woman's suffrage wouldn't just affect the voting booths and the halls of government, they knew. If women were more empowered to voice their opinions, who knew what would come next? Women might start making more demands for fair treatment and equal pay at their jobs, for equal opportunity in their careers, and for greater roles in their places of worship. They might even want to run for office! Girls might start speaking up in classrooms or wanting to play sports, go to college, or enlist in the military. Women would become more . . . *visible.*

America had been through more than enough changes in the past fifty years. The threat of woman's suffrage was the last thing the country needed, the Antis believed.

During World War I, women had been forced—or had the chance, depending on how you saw it—to take on traditionally masculine jobs. It was insane for women to try to join the world of men, the Antis preached. Suffrage was sure to bring about a "sex war" between husbands and wives, men and women, boys and girls. Arguments about politics would tear families—and the whole country—apart!

Then there was the issue of race. During the war, black men had served in the military, and black women had worked on the home front. They had helped America during a difficult time, and they demanded equality and respect for it. Of course, since 1916, black people had been leaving the South in droves, heading north in the first waves of the Great Migration. Demeaning Jim Crow segregation laws and vile threats of harassment, violence, and lynching by the Ku Klux Klan were unbearable. Those who stayed in the South demanded dignified jobs and pay, better houses and neighborhoods, and improved schools. And now, if woman's suffrage passed, black women would be allowed to vote, too? It made the southern Antis froth with rage.

Besides catering to white southerners' racism, Josephine, Charlotte, and the other Antis had another hot-button issue on their agenda: states' rights. Tennesseans were very concerned about their rights to make their own laws—without the interference of other states or the federal government. After the Civil War, they felt that their own state's rights had been trampled on. Ever since, politicians in Tennessee were protective of their right to govern their own people. How dare the American government force woman's suffrage onto individual states? Let New York and California and Illinois and Wyoming have their so-called New Women—those liberated types—the Antis argued, but leave be everyone else.

Basically, the Antis were trying to reach as wide an audience as they possibly could. Their message was loud and clear: If you don't want women—black or white—voting, we welcome you. If you approve of woman's suffrage but oppose the federal amendment trampling on states' rights, we also welcome you.

The response was highly enthusiastic.

The Suffs knew that the Antis' racial prejudices would worm their way into the argument. Anyone could have seen it coming from a mile away. Race has always been significant to all aspects of American life—and especially to the right to vote.

The woman's suffrage movement unfolded during a time of severe racial segregation, especially in the South, but also in many northern cities. Most suffrage clubs were segregated, with separate clubs for white and black women working for the Cause. The credo of the national movement was getting the vote for *all* women. But there is evidence that the woman's suffrage movement did not always welcome black women.

Abby Milton, the president of the Tennessee League of Women Voters, and Catherine Kenny wanted to change that. In May 1920, just a few months before the ratification vote would eventually take place, and in the very same capitol building, they had invited Mrs. Juno Frankie Pierce, an active suffragist and a founder of the Nashville Federation of Colored Women's Clubs,* to speak to the newly established Tennessee League of Women Voters.

Frankie stood tall, undaunted by the monumental statehouse. Abby and Catherine fixed their eyes on her as she spoke. All three women liked the idea of joining forces—white and black women—for the good of the community. This was, they believed, an example of what women's participation in government could accomplish.

"What will the Negro woman do with the vote?" Frankie asked her audience of several hundred white women, letting the question hang in the air.* Then she answered her own question with an air of calm authority: "Yes, we will stand by the white women. We are interested in the same

---

* "Colored" and "Negro" were once common terms used to describe African Americans but are now considered dated and offensive because of their historical association with segregation.

moral uplift of the community in which we live as you are," she explained. "We are asking only one thing—a square deal."

Frankie was proposing a partnership between black and white women to achieve their shared goal. "We want recognition in all forms of this government," Frankie said. "We want a state  vocational school, and a child welfare department of the state, and more room in state schools."

But Frankie was posing another question, urgent but unspoken, to her audience that morning: Will you, the white suffragists of Tennessee, stand by the black women of the state who also need to vote? Will you stand up for us when black women, like black men, are threatened and assaulted at the polls? Will you allow us to actually use the vote that we, like you, have been fighting for for so long? Those questions remained unanswered.

7 ★ CRANKING THE MACHINE

"*I* have come to help you win the thirty-sixth state," Carrie Catt announced to the women and men gathered in her Nashville hotel room. She'd called them in for a pep talk. Everyone was buzzing with excitement and nerves as they settled in. The very idea of "winning" Tennessee was supremely optimistic, Carrie knew, but she'd always liked to view her glass as half-full.

Like an army commander, Carrie stood straight-backed before her Suff troops. Feeling everyone's eyes on her, she issued her first orders:

Visit each legislator. Demand he sign the pledge to support ratification. Too many legislators are holding back. Be prepared for a few nos along the way. Don't let that stop you. Just keep going!

With a shudder, Carrie remembered Catherine's poll

from her first morning in Nashville. So many legislators had not responded—or had refused to reveal where they stood.

"That unheard from number can and may defeat the ratification," Catt told the Suffs. *Go back and find them, go knock on their doors*, she ordered. *Tennessee's friends of suffrage need to be shaken awake. The clock is ticking!*

The hotel room erupted in cheers. They could do it, they assured her.

Throughout Carrie's life, she'd witnessed the attitudes toward woman's suffrage change ever so slowly. Its supporters had been beaten down so many times.

Suffrage hasn't been defeated, Carrie had always insisted whenever they faced hardship. It's only been postponed.

Everything the Cause had accomplished—every state won, every piece of legislation, every change of heart and shift in policy—was once considered utterly impossible. Until it wasn't. The trick was to create a positive atmosphere, Carrie believed. Set an ambitious goal, then build your own highway to reach it.

If things looked iffy in Tennessee, she would never admit it in public. She would appear 100 percent optimistic. Hope was very motivating.

★　★　★

All over Tennessee, women could be seen roaming the countryside, hunting down legislators. The Suffs had to convince these men that ratifying the woman's suffrage amendment was the best thing for their state and for America. The Antis, meanwhile, were at their heels, trying to convince legislators of just the opposite message.

With the vote on ratification just weeks away, there wasn't a moment to lose.

Some women traveled by train to small towns to find their delegates. Others were carried in wagons down winding roads to isolated farmsteads, their dresses trailing in the mud. They were drenched by rainstorms, chased by watchdogs, and stranded by flat tires. But they found their men.

Carrie decided that she, Marjorie, and Tennessee suffrage leader Abby Milton would travel together throughout the state. Carrie knew her speeches were the absolute best way to get a crowd excited—even in the roasting heat.

Carrie Catt's first speech in Tennessee was on Friday, July 23, at Nashville's Commercial Club. Milling around the club's elegant dining room, she saw the friends and clients of Nashville's most powerful men shaking hands and chuckling with one another. They probably weren't used to quieting down and listening to a *woman*. It was up to her to win them over, show them that ratification was in their best interests, too—not just women's.

Carrie's speaking talents were famous. Secretly, though, even after all her experience talking to crowds, her stomach did backflips whenever she took the stage. She'd calm herself by clasping and unclasping her hands behind her back, twiddling her fingers. Only people sitting behind could ever see. Her audiences never knew.

A ceiling fan whirled overhead, circulating the musky scent of tobacco smoke around the room. Nervous as she was, Carrie still felt relieved to see how many men had turned up. The club was packed. Reporters from the *Nashville Tennessean* and the *Nashville Banner* opened their notebooks and poised their pens. Seated in the audience was Major Edward Bushrod Stahlman, publisher of the newspaper the *Banner*. He turned in his chair to listen.

Edward was a Big Man around Nashville. He had once been an executive in the L&N railroad company. Though he no longer worked for the railroad, he still advocated for their interests in the editorial pages of the *Banner*—and railroad interests held a lot of sway over the city's politics. As the publisher of a major newspaper, he could make or break a candidate or cause with his little finger. Many mayors, governors, and senators throughout the South feared him.

He didn't mind having enemies, though; all important men made enemies—it was a mark of power, he believed.

Carrie Catt peered out at the crowd and took a deep breath to calm her nerves. Chin held high, she stepped up to the podium.

She didn't beat around the bush. She spoke confidently and directly, in terms the men could readily understand: Ratifying the suffrage amendment was the best thing for Tennessee. Rejecting it, on the other hand, would be bad for business *and* for Nashville's future.

Besides, she noted, both presidential candidates were pushing for ratification. Why let them down? This was a glorious opportunity for America, for democracy! Shouldn't Tennesseans stand together, men and women, and push this amendment through?

The crowd burst into applause. Carrie knew she'd pulled it off.

Major Edward Stahlman approached Carrie to introduce himself, his cane rapping toward her. Even at seventy-seven years old he was an energetic man, with strong features and a head of snowy hair. He gave her his word: Governor Roberts and ratification had his full sup-port. The suffragists could count on him. Carrie grinned and thanked him. Everyone knew that Edward Stahlman was the kind of man you wanted on your side.

Following this first appearance, Carrie got an idea. Why not set this campaign off with a bang and give the Suffs a boost of good publicity? She and Marjorie Shuler quickly wrote a press release, declaring that ratification was basi-cally clinched. Sure, it was too early to be certain, but Car-rie was willing to make the leap. It was blue-sky optimism, and she was an optimist.

On Sunday night, July 25, Carrie, Marjorie, and Abby Milton dashed to Union Station to catch the overnight train to Memphis. Their press release would appear in the papers the very next morning. Carrie hoped it would make a splash.

Darkness blanketed the sky as the three women lay back in their sleeping cars that evening, rocked by the gentle rhythm of the train. But sleep wouldn't come to them. Their minds were weighed down with worry. It wasn't just because that press release they'd written was a tad exag-gerated. That morning the *Banner* had published an attack letter written by Anti leader Nina Pinckard aimed at Carrie Catt. It accused Carrie of forcing women into the "turmoil" of politics against their wills. It also accused her of trying to destroy white, southern traditions by speaking out about votes for *all* women.

Publishing the letter sure was a strange way for Major Edward Stahlman's paper to express its "full support" for the woman's suffrage amendment. . . .

8 ★ PRISON PIN

Sue White was running on pure adrenaline. Her nerves jangled and her mind was racing. If only her friends Betty Gram and Anita Pollitzer would arrive in Nashville already! Sue couldn't wait to see her fellow Woman's Party members. They always made the tough work feel like fun.

They each had a lot of ground to cover, winning over the men who pulled the strings around Nashville. Sue's knowledge of her home state would be very useful.

Before Sue left her hotel room, she pushed the sharp point of a pin through her blouse and fastened it on. The small silver rectangle was the most special thing she owned. She'd earned it after she was arrested the year before. Alice Paul had given all the women a pin after they got arrested, in thanks for taking such big risks for the Cause.

As Sue gazed out her hotel window onto the busy Nashville streets, she remembered that exciting day in

Washington, D.C. It had been February 1919. The Senate was *finally* going to vote on the federal suffrage amendment. Of course, no one expected it to pass. It was one measly vote short. President Wilson had been in Paris negotiating the peace treaty at the time. He didn't exactly seem to mind letting the woman's suffrage amendment die.

That's where Alice Paul had stepped in. She and the Woman's Party had already been protesting outside the White House, lighting small bonfires and burning the president's words about democracy. On the eve of the Senate vote, she and her troops *really* turned up the heat.

At dusk, a silent procession of seventy-five women, including Sue, had marched toward the White House. Leading the parade was Woman's Party member Louisine Havemeyer, holding the American flag. Women propped up banners saying things like, "The President is responsible for the betrayal of American Womanhood." Others followed, carrying kerosene-soaked wooden logs and kindling in their arms.

Almost two thousand people and a hundred policemen had gathered in front of the White House gates to watch. They weren't quite sure what to expect from these rebellious women.

Louisine, who was a wealthy New York widow, planted her flag. Her heart was beating wildly, she would later tell the Woman's Party members, but once she stepped out with the flag, she "instantly felt as placid and calm as if I were going out to play croquet on a summer afternoon."

At the White House gates, her booming voice had risen above the crowd: "We women of America are assembled here today to voice our deep indignation that, while such efforts are being made to establish democracy in Europe, American women are still deprived of a voice in their government here at home."

While Louisine spoke, the logs were lit. The flames rose high. Sue knew this was her moment. She stepped up to the fire and held up over her head a paper figure of President Wilson drawn in black ink. It depicted him delivering one of those empty "freedom" speeches of his. Sue nodded to Louisine. Then she dropped the Wilson image into the flames.

There was a flash. Chaos broke loose. Police rushed toward the women, spraying them with fire extinguishers and arresting as many protesters as they could. They grabbed Sue and shoved her straight into a patrol wagon. She found herself next to Louisine and thirty-seven other Woman's Party members. Before they knew it, they were driven straight to the station house.

Five days in jail, the policemen thundered, for each of them. The Occoquan Workhouse was a decrepit, nasty-smelling, vermin-infested jail. The women entered dark, damp, bitter cold cells. Rats and cockroaches scurried on every surface. Still, the conditions were better, and the sentences much shorter, than the six- and seven-month ordeals, often in solitary confinement, that Alice Paul had suffered through.

When Sue and the others were released after their five-day sentence, they were welcomed home by their Woman's Party comrades. Alice Paul held a small ceremony to give them their prison pins. The pin was a miniature of a jail door gridded by little silver bars, draped with a chain of tiny links, secured by a heart-shaped lock. Every woman who was "jailed for freedom" was decorated with one. No piece of jewelry could ever mean more to Sue White.

When Sue's Tennessee suffrage colleagues had heard she'd been arrested, they were furious. She was going to give suffragists a bad name, they cried. Protesting the president was unpatriotic, even treasonous!

Sue had rolled her eyes. She didn't care what those goody-two-shoes NAWSA women thought. She and her Woman's Party comrades understood the power of fighting against injustice. She believed *they* were the true daughters of Susan B. Anthony.

Suddenly, Sue snapped out of her memory haze. She switched off the lights in her Nashville hotel room before dashing down to the lobby to meet her next batch of legislators. Sure, she knew it was a little bold to wear her prison pin in Tennessee. But she would wear it nonetheless: brazenly, proudly, every day.

At just twenty-five years old, Anita Pollitzer was already an experienced veteran of the radical Woman's Party.

Anita was an artist who'd traded her brushes for picket poles. Unlike many young women who joined the movement, her family was actually very proud of her work. She was the adored daughter of a wealthy Charleston, South Carolina, cotton merchant family, pillars of the city's thriving Jewish community.

Anita grew up assuming that being a suffragist was only natural for a young woman. Supporting women's rights was just so *obvious,* she felt. She was smart, fun, creative, and courageous, just like all the girls she knew. Why should boys get all the spotlight? From a young age, she did everything she could to spread the word on woman's suffrage, from drawing recruitment posters, to selling lemonade to raise money, to debating Antis in the street.

When the ratification campaign began, Alice Paul often sent Anita to Washington, D.C. It was hard for congressmen and senators to say no to her. She was charming and charismatic, and she really did her homework before approaching them. She sweetly asked questions. She listened carefully.

But she learned pretty quickly not to trust any politician's promise. They would agree to things to your face, then break their promises once you turned your back. The petite Anita might *appear* innocent, but gullibility was not one of her traits.

Anita loved the work. It was so exciting! Like being a soldier and a spy rolled into one. Her job was to find things out and shake things up. She could hardly wait to see her friends Sue White and Betty Gram, now that they'd all be working on the big amendment push in Tennessee. They had an easy understanding, a sisterly bond, an unspoken trust. Best of all, they could make each other laugh—something that could come in handy if things got stressful.

As part of this latest push, Anita's first stop on the Tennessee trail was Chattanooga to meet Newell Sanders, a former U.S. senator and loyal suffragist. He sat Anita down at his kitchen table and spent the afternoon giving her a crash course in Tennessee Republican politics.

He told her everything he knew: which men called the shots, which men were rivals, which ones had a vulnerable spot. Newell also pointed out which men might try to dodge her and which ones might cause trouble. She listened attentively, fixing her gray eyes upon him, scribbling notes down in a notebook on her lap. This was all really helpful information for her next stops. She shook Newell's hand and thanked him with a grin.

Anita's manhunt continued through the Appalachian foothills of East Tennessee. When she stepped off the train in Athens, the McMinn County seat, she went after the area's pivotal players, one by one.

There was Senator Herschel Candler, who was anti-suffrage *and* powerful, a tough combination. Herschel had already made his stance crystal clear: "I unalterably oppose suffrage and shall vote against the bill," he'd announced with his trademark stubbornness. But Anita reached out anyway. All she got back from him was: *Cannot vote for amendment. Period.* Anita groaned and crossed his name off her list. Well, forget that Herschel Candler.

Next, she hired a car to see Emerson Luther, the Republican house floor leader, and came away with his pledge. The delegate C. Fulton Boyer was next on her list, but he was known as a cranky old Anti—probably not even worth her time. She decided to skip him.

That left the last man on her list: Harry T. Burn.

At twenty-four years old, representative Harry Burn was the youngest member of the legislature. He was, according to everyone, likable, sweet, and hardworking. He was a hometown boy making good, living on his family's land, supporting his widowed mother and his siblings. Like many other representatives, he had a day job outside of politics. In fact, he worked two jobs, one as a Southern Railway agent, the other at a bank, while studying law at night. That hard-working Harry Burn had the potential to go far, his peers all agreed.

Harry had voted for limited suffrage the year before. But he was keeping his cards close to his chest when it came to ratification. The Suffs thought he was being a little shady. Why not just say yes or no?

Anita quickly realized that speaking face to face with Harry Burn wasn't going to be easy. She couldn't afford a taxi to get to Harry's small hometown. So  she did the next best thing: she sweetly asked a Republican county chairman if he'd be so kind as to telephone Harry for her. No problem, the chairman agreed. Anita waited patiently as he dialed Harry's number.

Lady here wants to know if you'll be voting to ratify, Harry, the chairman said into the phone's mouthpiece. Anita strained to hear Harry's response through the muffled sounds. She couldn't make it out.

The conversation was brief. The chairman hung the phone back on its cradle.

Harry will be all right, the chairman assured her.

Anita ticked his name off on her list. And with that, Harry T. Burn was marked as pledged to ratify.

9 ★ FIELDWORK

*T*he dog days of summer were usually a peaceful time in Tennessee. Quiet nights sitting out on porches. Family picnics, followed by naps under a shady tree. That kind of thing. Not so much this year. Suffragists and Antis were zigzagging across the state in a frenzy, trying to keep calm and cool under the blazing southern sun.

Carrie Catt was giving rallying speeches throughout Tennessee, from Memphis to Knoxville to Chattanooga. Sue White was racing around Nashville, snagging important legislators. Josephine Pearson was planning Anti meetings around Nashville. Meanwhile, Charlotte Rowe fanned the Anti flames across the state.

Everyone was in motion.

Before radio or television or the internet, this was how the suffragists got the word out about their mission. Door-to-door. Town-to-town. For decades, women had pleaded for the vote. They had protested, petitioned, and been jailed again and again. Now they were back in the field for the final stage, with both Suffs and Antis scrambling to win. The clock was ticking.

Like an impatient fisherman, Sue wanted to reel in Seth Walker *fast*. Seth was the slippery sort, but he was an essential catch. As Speaker of the house in Tennessee, his role gave him all sorts of powers that he could use to help—or destroy—the passage of the woman's suffrage amendment.

Seth Walker was an Albert Roberts supporter. He sided with the governor on just about everything. Tall, good-looking, and just twenty-eight years old, he had a reputation as a clever lawyer and had quickly moved up in the world of politics. All the way up to the role of Speaker of Tennessee's house of representatives. He also served as an attorney for the Nashville, Chattanooga, and St. Louis Railway, which paid him very well.

During the limited suffrage debate last year, Seth had surprised everyone by changing his mind on limited suffrage—first he opposed it, then suddenly switched and supported it. He flip-flopped with no explanation. The Suffs weren't exactly sure why, but they were pleased by it.

But now that the chance to give women *full* suffrage had

come around, he was hesitating. The Suffs were getting a little impatient with him. He was a man whom others followed. But he hadn't responded to the poll, he hadn't sent in his pledge, and he wasn't answering any messages. Sue worried he'd swallowed the Antis' bait.

Sue wasn't ready to give up on Seth yet, though. She badgered him nonstop, popping into his office, listing all the reasons to ratify.

Finally, in the very last days of July, he agreed to support the amendment. When Sue heard the news, she instantly wired Alice Paul and called Anita Pollitzer, whooping with delight.

She even spilled the beans to the newspapers, to make it official.

Betty Gram slipped into Memphis to begin her mission. Betty had dreamed of being an actress and singer but gave up the stage for a part in the suffrage movement with the radical Woman's Party. As charming as she was fierce, Betty was also clever, courageous, and not a bit intimidated by powerful men. If unsuspecting legislators simply saw her as a pretty face, they'd better think twice.

Betty wasn't shy about being a "militant." Like her friend Sue, she wore her prison pin with pride. In Memphis, she unpacked her bag, shook out her hair, and got straight to work scheduling meetings with important men.

Betty and the Woman's Party were trying to get legislators to clearly say: *If elected, I will vote to ratify the federal suffrage amendment.* Soon enough, Betty came away with the pledge of Joseph Hanover, a well-dressed thirty-year-old Memphis delegate. He was eager to help ratify the amendment to give women the vote.

Another big score for the Suffs was a pledge from Thomas Riddick. Thomas was a Memphis attorney and had been supporting women's rights for a while now. The Suffs knew they could trust him.

Between Joe Hanover and Tom Riddick, they felt they had at least two important men solidly in their corner.

By the latest Woman's Party count, the Suffs were ten votes short in the house and six votes short in the senate. They were desperate to get more men on their side.

But across the state from Betty Gram, fellow Woman's Party member Anita Pollitzer started to notice something strange: many of the legislators she approached seemed more and more skittish at the mention of woman's suffrage. They'd avoid her, ignore her questions, or answer in a vague, noncommittal way. Even the ones who had already pledged!

Anita and the Woman's Party Suffs weren't the only ones to notice this pattern. The NAWSA Suffs were noticing it, too. As Carrie moved from town to town, her smiles and speeches started to feel a bit strained. Her rosy mood was darkening. The Antis were up to some dirty tricks, and word was getting around fast.

Newspaper stories about Charlotte Rowe sweeping into town or Nina Pinckard cozying up to lawmakers were one thing. A *double agent* working with the Antis was quite another one. Apparently, a powerful Tennessee Republican was pretending to work for ratification—then passing the Suffs' secrets on to the Antis. And plenty of legislators who'd agreed to vote for woman's suffrage were now changing their minds.

These two-timing politicians! Carrie felt sick with anger.

Presidential candidate Warren G. Harding's name was in the news again, the Suffs noticed with a grimace. This time, he seemed to be distancing himself from his pro-ratification stance. He was refusing to comment on ratification in Tennessee at all.

Harding's patience was seriously fraying. He was being bothered by all sides: those pushy Suffs, the persistent Antis, lawyers, journalists, and now Tennessee Republicans, too.

The national election was only thirteen weeks away. He was trying to become president! And all anyone was thinking about was Tennessee and women voting.

Focus, he told himself. He had to seem serious. Impressive. Presidential. If he could avoid saying anything too controversial for the next few weeks, he might be able to beat that dull Democrat James Cox and win the White House.

Recently, Harding and Cox had received identical letters from the Tennessee Constitutional League. The men in the league were strictly Anti. Their message was crystal clear: keep your "hands off" our state, they demanded. The threatening tone didn't escape Harding's attention. He felt relieved that he'd decided to keep his neck out of Tennessee. Those Suff women weren't his problem anyway.

At noon on Wednesday, August 4, Carrie Catt was scheduled to give a talk at Chattanooga's swanky Hotel Patten. The audience was an impressive bunch of political powerhouses. Carrie was usually nervous about public speaking, but something felt different this time. She was tired of politicians and their weak excuses for keeping women down.

All that frustration was driving her forward. She was too angry to even feel nervous.

Carrie approached the podium with her head high, her tone loud and bold as she began speaking.

The Constitutional League, the men's Anti group, does not "appear to be behind the opposition," she declared, "but when they send to Cox and Harding messages to 'leave Tennessee alone' you may know it is this little band . . . who are behind it." Carrie presented her evidence like it was a detective story, turning her magnifying glass on the Constitutional League. Reporters scribbled furiously in their notebooks.

"The opponents of suffrage are trying to fool the people of Tennessee," Carrie fumed. She was speaking with an unfiltered fury that even her closest friends had never heard before.

Any delay in approving the amendment, she continued, would "pass into history as a testimonial to the stupidity of Tennessee."

The crowd gasped and murmured disapprovingly. At the back of the room, Marjorie Shuler and Abby Milton cringed. Had Carrie really just called Tennessee stupid? It was so out of character for her! Clearly all that stress she'd felt during the past several weeks, the bitter frustration she'd bottled up, was now bubbling out.

"Go to see your representatives and senators, and set them right!" Carrie thundered, then strode away from the podium.

The next evening, Carrie, Marjorie, and Abby took the train back to Nashville. Carrie didn't say much on the ride. She just wanted to get back to her hotel room and be alone for a while.

When Carrie's remarks reached Josephine Pearson and the Tennessee Antis, they were furious. How *dare* this Yankee come onto their turf and insult them?

They weren't offended for long, though. Mostly they were amused. They saw Carrie's speech as proof that the Suffs felt themselves slipping, losing their grip.

And the Antis weren't wrong.

10 ★ WAR OF THE ROSES

*O*n Saturday afternoon, August 7, Governor Albert Roberts officially called the General Assembly to meet in special session. The session would start on Monday at noon. The suffrage confrontation—anticipated, relished, dreaded—was finally set. It would begin in less than forty-eight hours.

All over Tennessee, men of the legislature began packing their bags, kissing their wives and children good-bye, and boarding steam trains headed for Nashville. No one could tell how long they'd be gone. It could be just a few days or as long as three weeks (the full term of the session).

The moment they reached Union Station, welcoming parties of women pounced on them.

Here! Suffs cried out, shoving yellow roses at the men. *Take these!*

Take these *instead!* Antis shouted over the Suffs, thrusting red roses at the men's suit lapels, trying to pin them on.

Yellow or gold had long been the American suffrage campaign's hue, while the Antis had adopted a patriotic red. Newspapers were already calling this battle over suffrage "the Tennessee War of the Roses."

Suffragists used colors to bring attention to their movement. They often wore white dresses with yellow sashes in their public demonstrations. To them, yellow and gold represented the sun, a new day dawning for women. White represented purity of purpose. The Woman's Party added other symbolic colors to their displays: purple for loyalty and green for hope.

Over that August weekend, the lobby of the Hotel Hermitage was the place to be. Groups of Suffs, Antis, and legislators all gathered to meet, talk, or confront each other. The grandeur of the space—its marble columns and painted ceilings, the plush carpets below and shimmering chandeliers above—gave a sense of both seriousness and festivity.

By Saturday afternoon, the lobby was humming with conversation. The sounds of juicy gossip, business conversations, and heated arguments could be heard at every corner. Sun rays slanted through the painted-glass skylight, illuminating the feathered and flowered hats of ladies and the linen suits of gentlemen.

The Antis were descending upon Nashville with a vengeance. Mary Kilbreth, president of the National Association Opposed to Woman Suffrage, arrived from New York City. Laura Clay of Kentucky and Kate Gordon from New Orleans—the former suffragists who'd changed their tunes—were expected soon.

Together, the Antis reviewed their main talking points. They had to make convincing arguments to any legislators who were still on the fence about woman's suffrage. And if any Antis forgot their main points, Josephine Pearson was there to remind them.

Remember the issues at stake in this fight, she crowed to a group of men and women who'd just arrived at the Hermitage:

The threat that the federal amendment poses to our states' rights.

The frightening potential of racial equality if black women and men are allowed to vote.

And the "war of the sexes" that suffrage will surely unfold between men and "liberated" women who do not know their places.

Then, with a winning smile, she passed out a red rose

to each of them. The number of Anti red roses seemed to multiply every minute.

The polished wooden doors of Anti headquarters swung open at exactly five o'clock that Saturday afternoon for a welcome party. All the legislators, the members of the Constitutional League, and the Antis of Nashville had been invited. Josephine Pearson's southern hospitality made everyone feel at home. She greeted her guests with a smile, all the while keeping everyone's punch glass filled and the cookie trays stacked high. She was in her element.

The reception was more than just a way to greet the legislators. Nina Pinckard had also organized something special: an anti-ratification exhibit for the crowd to wander through. The exhibit was full of provocative artifacts that showed the immorality of the suffragists. If the Suffs didn't already have a bad enough reputation in the South, the Antis were about to make it even worse.

There were photographs of Susan B. Anthony's black friends. There were Anti brochures and posters warning that ratification would "re-open the horrors of Reconstruction" when black men voted and even served in the legislature.

But the highlight of the exhibition was a dusty old book:

Elizabeth Cady Stanton's *Woman's Bible*. It had been a huge bestseller in 1895—and a big headache for the Suffs ever since. Elizabeth's main points—that the Bible wasn't the Divine Word of God, but a creation by men to keep women down—had been causing a stir ever since it was published. Antis called it the work of Satan. Now they were labeling it "Mrs. Catt's Bible" (which was also a huge stretch).

Nearly two hundred guests milled through the room. They admired the posters and brochures, then clucked their tongues at the copy of *The Woman's Bible*. Josephine tapped her glass and stood on a small platform to thank everyone for coming. Nina Pinckard, Charlotte Rowe, and Mary Kilbreth spoke next.

Let's defeat this amendment—together! they cried out to the cheering audience.

Just a few flights above, the Suffs winced at the idea of the Antis' "exhibit." For the most part, they stayed in their hotel rooms. Only occasionally did they send spies into the lobby. It couldn't hurt to eavesdrop on the enemy.

11 ★ SHAKEN UP

$\mathcal{E}$arly on Sunday morning, August 8, Governor Albert Roberts's aides bounded up the steps of the capitol building, briefcases in hand. House Speaker Seth Walker would be meeting with them in just a few minutes. The governor really needed Seth's help keeping the Antis at bay. It was time to nail down a win for woman's suffrage, once and for all.

Between the election in November and the fight for suffrage in Nashville, Albert was under a lot of pressure. He still had to win the general election and beat Republican Alf Taylor. Alf was serious competition. His numbers in the election polls were starting to creep up.

If Albert had any hope of holding on to his job as the governor of Tennessee, he'd need help. Specifically, the help of the Democratic presidential candidate: James Cox.

But *first*, Albert knew that he would need to prove to

Cox that the suffrage amendment was a sure bet in Tennes-see. Woman's suffrage would be good for the Democratic Party, Cox believed. He wouldn't give Albert a hand unless it ratified.

Besides, Albert also could really use the votes of Ten-nessee women. Surely if he stood by their side, they'd be grateful enough to him to mark his name on the ballot. Or so he hoped.

Albert's closest advisers were still strongly against ratifi-cation. His support for it would ruin his career, they warned. All the Tennesseans pushing for states' rights would be mad at him. Worse yet, the powerful corporations and businesses of Tennessee saw woman's suffrage as nothing but a wrench in their plans to make more money.

Yes, Albert had admitted to his advisers, these were all solid points. But he overruled them. Albert knew what he had to do: he had to push this ratification through the legis-lature, no matter what! So what if he angered a few people? His career, in the long run, depended on it. And he had the whole thing set up: the Speaker of the house, Seth Walker, had the power to carry the amendment in the house; senate Speaker Andrew Todd would guide it through the senate. Albert had his team.

Seth Walker was on board for ratification: he'd joined the Men's Ratification Committee and pledged to vote aye.

He was even going to be the one to introduce the ratification resolution in the house of representatives. The game plan needed to be perfected before it was put in play tomorrow, even though everything was basically in place.

That's why it was such a shock to Governor Roberts's team when Seth marched in to their meeting, flushed and agitated. He'd had a "change of conviction," he announced. He'd decided to oppose ratification. And, he said, Governor Roberts was courting political disaster if he continued to support it.

With that, Seth turned on his heel and strode out the door.

Albert Roberts and his staff were shell-shocked. What on earth were they going to do now? Everything—the reputation of the Democratic Party, the upcoming election, not to mention getting all those radical Suff ladies off his back—depended on a quick, easy ratification. Albert tried to reason with Seth, practically begging him to reconsider. But the young lawyer's mind was set. Whatever—or whoever—could have changed his mind?

By evening, the governor's normally scowling face—he rarely smiled—took on a look of total dismay. Albert knew he had to keep a lid on all this, to keep it hidden from the newspapers as long as possible. It was embarrassing! It made him look like he wasn't in control of his allies, let alone the whole legislature. His weakness was showing. How could he explain this to Cox? Or to President Wilson?

He needed time to think things through, to come up with an alternate plan. But—now that the city was crawling with politicians and journalists—this had to be the worst time to try to keep a secret.

That evening, Governor Roberts had a meeting with Tennessee Suffs in the executive wing of the statehouse. With just a few hours until the session, they had to cram to review last-minute strategies. Albert was extremely impressed by how prepared the women were. They seemed to know as much as his team—more, even. He promised the women he'd do everything in his power to win ratification.

He just didn't tell them that Seth Walker had deserted them, double-crossed him, and made the whole ratification business much more difficult. It was up to Seth to tell them that himself.

Carrie Catt knew that Harriet Upton had arrived at the Hotel Hermitage when she heard a booming laugh echo down the hallway. That was Harriet's distinct laugh, all right, and Carrie was happy to hear it. Carrie and Harriet had been working together on the Cause for thirty years. They'd both been Aunt Susan's girls. Harriet was comfortable with the rough-and-tumble of politics. She didn't mind getting her hands dirty or cracking jokes to lighten up any awkward situations.

Carrie was thrilled to see her comrade. Harriet was also an "outsider," another Yankee fish-out-of-water in the South. Carrie was just beginning to realize how much southerners resented the meddling of the out-of-town Suffs. Between Nina Pinckard's nasty smear piece in the *Banner* and the dirty looks Carrie got in the halls of the hotel, these Antis were having a fine time picking on her.

On Sunday night, with the opening of the special session just hours away, the Chief gathered her troops. NAWSA Suffs of all stripes—women and men, Democrats and Republicans—assembled in Carrie's Hermitage suite. Harriet Upton and Marjorie Shuler joined, too.

Carrie was all business. The Antis would be throwing every possible obstacle into the amendment's path, she knew. She had to prepare her warriors to win.

Their strategy was all set. Carrie broke it down once more:

Maintain pressure on the presidential candidates and national parties.

Keep close tabs on the legislators.

Push for a quick ratification vote—before any more men could be swayed by the Antis.

The Suffs listened closely, nodding in agreement. Passing the amendment was their number one goal, but making the Chief proud was a close second.

They'd spent the past weekend diligently socializing, greeting delegates at the train station, and chatting them up in the Hermitage lobby. Drama was heating up, though. Some men were changing their minds or trying to pledge both ways! Others were planning to not vote at all. And now the newspapers were filled with stories about "mysterious influences" and "vague, nameless forces" entering Nashville. These "forces," the papers claimed, were "reputed to have the unlimited financial backing of certain interests, which are opposed on principle . . . to woman suffrage." Translation: big businesses, such as the L&N Railroad, were trying to influence men to vote *against* woman's suffrage.

Carrie brushed the Suffs' worries away and tried to keep their spirits bright. She dove into the details of the battle plan, speaking with confidence and force:

Only Tennessee NAWSA women—like Abby Milton, Anne Dudley, Catherine Kenny, and Charl Williams—were to go to the statehouse, Carrie said. They would present a 100 percent Tennessean face in the capitol. Carrie and Harriet would stay in the background. They wouldn't go to the statehouse at all, so their "Yankee" presence wouldn't play into the Antis' hands.

Meanwhile, Sue's plan was to be right out there on the firing line, on the floor of the chambers. She also needed her fellow Woman's Party members, especially Anita Pollitzer and Betty Gram, to guard their assigned men. The three of them were trying hard to seem cool and calm, the model Woman's Party warriors. But they struggled to hide their terror.

None of the Suffs knew of Seth Walker's betrayal yet.

Their strategy sessions ran long and late. Around midnight, the Suffs all parted ways to go to bed. Few could sleep.

12 ★ IN JUSTICE TO WOMANHOOD

$\mathcal{A}$ ll through the weekend, porters had been cleaning and polishing the statehouse. Floors were mopped. Desks were dusted. Cobwebs were swept away.

On Monday morning, the doors of the capitol swung open for the first time in months. Suffs and Antis bustled through, their arms full of decorations. Both sides wanted to spruce up the halls, brighten the place up with their own colors and roses. Suffs tacked yellow bunting and banners to the walls and railings. Antis lugged boxes of artificial red roses up the grand marble staircase.

The visitor galleries above the chamber floors were packed. Clusters of women filled the doorways. The statehouse had never seen so much excitement. Hordes of women in the capitol? Flowers everywhere? Some men couldn't believe their eyes. Quite a few seemed to like it just fine.

No matter which way you looked at it, the War of the Roses had begun.

Shortly past noon, Seth Walker pounded his gavel. The house of representatives came to order.

At the exact same time, on the south side of the capitol, Andrew Todd rapped his gavel. The Tennessee Senate came to order, too.

The first order of the day was the Nineteenth Amendment. In a clear, loud voice, a clerk read the suffrage amendment aloud to each chamber: "The right of citizens of the United States to vote shall not be denied or abridged by the United States or by any State on account of sex."

Next, each clerk also read out a personal statement from Governor Albert Roberts himself.

Both Suffs and Antis held their breath. Neither side had any idea what to expect. To the Suffs' pleasant surprise, the governor's words were simple and straightforward. He urged the legislature to ratify the amendment—and to do it fast. "Tennessee occupies a pivotal position on this question," he reminded the delegates. "Millions of women are looking to the Tennessee legislature to give them a voice."

This was stronger stuff than the Suffs had expected. Albert Roberts's support of suffrage sounded urgent, even passionate.

Antis in the audience grimaced. *Traitor*, they whispered with disgust.

In the senate, Seth Walker leaned back in the leather Speaker's chair as he listened to the governor's words. His expression was calm. He didn't want to draw any attention to himself. At least, not yet. Few knew that he'd changed his mind on suffrage.

Before long, both chambers of the General Assembly adjourned until the next morning, taking no action on ratification. The Suffs groaned quietly. The legislators were really dragging this process out.

From her Hotel Hermitage window, Carrie could see women and men pouring out of the statehouse. She and Harriet had remained in her hotel suite, out of the public eye. Carrie had a strange feeling in her stomach. It bothered her that the legislators had adjourned so quickly. Were they taking the issue of suffrage seriously at *all*? They were dangling the vote over women's noses, like a carrot over a horse. It was humiliating!

And then there were all those mysterious men milling

around in the Hermitage lobby. She was told they were nothing more than slimy salesmen, trying to smooth-talk the legislators into smothering ratification. They'd sidle up to a legislator, lie about their names and jobs. They'd casually start pressing the Anti argument—then offer a sweet deal to anyone who came around to it.

On Monday evening, the Suffs breathlessly prepared for the next day's session. If there was one man whose help they could really use, it was Seth Walker's. The Suffs' latest poll numbers were slipping. Hopefully Seth would know just what to do. His insider knowledge of the legislature couldn't be beat.

Weirdly, the women couldn't find him anywhere. He wasn't responding to their calls. He wasn't in his office. When they finally tracked him down, his eyes were blazing. He kept jerking his head around, as if looking for the nearest exit.

He knew there was no hiding any longer. That's when he finally revealed himself.

No, he told the Suffs, he would *not* be sponsoring the ratification resolution at the statehouse. On top of that, he couldn't support—or vote for—ratification.

With that, he ran off. The Suffs didn't even have a

chance to respond, much less yell at him. Which is exactly what they felt like doing.

The shock of Seth's betrayal knocked them sideways. Sue White and Betty Gram could hardly believe it. He'd sworn to each of them that he would support the amendment. They had believed him! They'd been played.

In Carrie's room that night, the NAWSA Suffs met for a strategy meeting. As much as they tried to get down to business, it was impossible for anyone to concentrate. They couldn't get over that no-good, lying Seth Walker! But it wasn't just Seth—it was Governor Albert Roberts and James Cox. Both men *must* have known the Speaker was about to betray them, and neither lifted a finger to stop it! (Cox, in fact, hadn't known.)

Carrie tried to calm her women. *Focus!* she said. *We can recover from this.* The younger women were rattled, but Carrie had experienced this type of betrayal before. She was disgusted, but not exactly surprised.

It was a rough night and a raw morning for the bleary-eyed Suffs. And by breakfast, they were hit with yet another blow. Seth was now announcing that he intended to *lead* the opposition to the amendment on the house floor. He would "go down the line" to defeat the amendment, using his power as Speaker. And he was determined to bring as many house members with him as he could.

Josephine Pearson smirked when she heard the news. She put down her teacup and toast to devour all the juicy details she could from the morning paper. It made her giggle to imagine Carrie Catt's reaction to being betrayed.

The Antis could now officially call Seth Walker their friend.

Later that day, Betty Gram was crossing the Hermitage lobby to meet her Woman's Party friends when she noticed a suited man out of the corner of her eye. She knew that jacket. It was Seth Walker's.

Betty quickened her pace. She marched right up to him: Was it true that he was going to break his pledge to her and oppose ratification? she demanded. Seth whirled around, startled. The lobby hushed. Men and women craned their necks to see what was going on.

He recovered his wits: "I'd let the old Capitol crumble and fall from the hill before I'd vote for ratification," he said boastfully. "I'm going to do all I can to influence friends to vote No."

Betty snorted. "What has brought about the change against the suffrage amendment in the house—the governor or the Louisville and Nashville Railroad?" she demanded loudly. "What kind of a crook are you anyway—a Roberts crook or an L&N crook?"

Onlookers gasped.

"How dare you charge me with such a thing!" Seth bellowed. "That is an insult!"

Betty smiled and batted her lashes. "Why, I am just asking you for information," she replied with mock girlish innocence.

Seth stormed off, his hands clenched in his pockets.

Betty glared after him. It was a moment of sweet revenge. But it might have been costly.

That afternoon, reporters swarmed Carrie Catt, asking for her reaction to Seth's betrayal. Carrie tried to keep it breezy. No point in showing the papers how angry she *really* was.

Our polls are strong, she told them coolly. "I have absolute confidence in the integrity of the legislators of Tennessee and believe that they will stand by their pledges."

While Carrie faked confidence, Sue and her Woman's Party comrades were visibly worried. And now Woman's Party leader Alice Paul was sending them testy telegrams.

What is going on down there? Alice demanded. *Do we have a majority? Do you expect success?*

Sue caught her breath. It was up to her to hold down the fort while Alice worked in Washington. But what was Sue to do? Admit to Alice—her mentor, her hero—that she'd lost control of the campaign? Explain that support for ratification was mysteriously evaporating—all on her watch?

Sue willed herself to be calm, brave, and focused. She was smart and determined. She knew what she was doing! She just had to remind herself of that fact—and to live up to Alice Paul's trust in her.

The hottest gossip around Nashville on Tuesday was about Betty Gram's fiery confrontation with Seth Walker. Betty had insulted the Speaker, Seth's friends complained, and questioned his integrity. She must apologize, they insisted.

Betty Gram had no intention of apologizing. "We are not going to be thrust aside easily," she said defiantly. "Some sinister underground influence is at work here. We are entitled to know just who is changing a majority to a minority. If the liquor interests or the Louisville and Nashville railroad are responsible," Gram threatened, "we will find it out."

Seth was still shaking with rage after his spat with Betty Gram. That woman had tried to humiliate him! And in front of all those people, too. He knew he'd better come up with some sort of excuse for his new stance against the suffrage amendment. Fast.

"I have become convinced that it is my duty to my state and to my constituents to oppose this thing," he explained to a reporter for the *Chattanooga Times*. "There is no question in my mind that a large majority of the people, both men and women in Tennessee, are against universal suffrage from principles, or are violently opposed to action through a federal amendment."

But, the papers noticed, Seth didn't explain the suddenness of his "change of conviction." Nor did he bother mentioning all his money-making work on the side for the railroad company—the very railroad company that was famously anti-suffrage.

13 ★ DELAYS AHEAD

*O*n Wednesday morning during a session in the house of representatives, majority leader William Bond, a close friend of Seth Walker's, rose from his seat. Together, these two young lawyers were about to launch a sneaky ploy. If everything worked according to plan, there was no doubt they would delay any vote on suffrage.

As William stood before the chamber, the floor and galleries quieted. His job this morning was simple enough: to introduce a resolution, or proposal, to the house for all the men to vote on. But this resolution was actually a maneuver he and Seth had been working on—meant to delay and destroy ratification. Of course, he didn't present it that way. He presented it as the only sensible option for the state of Tennessee.

This legislature, William began, shouldn't take action on ratification until the voice of the people has been heard.

Both men and women, in every county of the state, should meet to discuss whether they even want the legislature to consider ratifying a suffrage amendment. These meetings would take place in two weeks' time. Then a chairman in each county would report the opinion of its citizens by August 24. Only then, William finished, could the legislators properly vote on behalf of their constituents.

The chamber erupted: shouts, cheers, and protests on the floor and in the galleries. Everyone was on their feet. Clearly, this plan would shatter any chance for timely ratification—or any ratification at all!

The Antis applauded. The Suffs booed: this ridiculous mass-meeting idea was a candy-coated excuse for legislators to do absolutely nothing.

A hot debate began on the floor; faces flushed and voices rose.

Both parties had *already* declared the need for ratification, said Leonidas (L. D.) Miller, a firm suffrage supporter. "And far and above the political party appeals," he cried, "comes the voice of the womanhood of America calling for justice long overdue." The Suffs in the gallery cheered. "To throw this question back upon the people will show cowardice," L. D. boomed.

Seth stepped down from the Speaker's chair and onto the floor to defend the Bond resolution. After all, it had partly been *his* idea. "We want to get an expression from the people!" Seth declared to red-rosed applause.

Josephine Pearson watched the argument from her gallery seat, her face flushed with excitement. She'd never seen anything like this. Her mentor, Mr. Vertrees, hadn't let her set foot in the statehouse during the 1917 and 1919 debates. Finally, she was seeing the legislature in action. Here were the brave Anti men of Tennessee taking their stand, upholding the honor of the South. She couldn't be prouder of them. Especially that young, very handsome Seth Walker.

Thomas Riddick, a close ally of the Suffs, jumped into the fray. This resolution was ridiculous, Thomas railed, his eyes blazing as he spoke. These so-called mass conventions couldn't possibly measure the people of Tennessee's views on woman's suffrage. How would their opinions be counted—by who showed up first? By who yelled the loudest? There was too much room for fraud!

Just then, Governor Roberts arrived in the chamber, sweating through his shirt and crumpled jacket. Immediately he started scribbling strategy notes, passing them on to delegates. Albert had just spoken with James Cox on the phone, had lied and told Cox things were under control. Now Albert had to actually *get* things under control.

Sue White and Anita Pollitzer, standing at the edge of the chamber, looked over at the governor suspiciously. They still suspected that he was double-dealing. *He's acting as if he's working for ratification,* Anita whispered to her friend, *but his own men are working against us.*

As the house debate wore on, Joe Hanover stood up. *I wish to speak against the Bond resolution,* he announced. The Suffs sat up a little straighter. They had high hopes for this bold, young attorney. During the past few nights, he'd joined in the Suffs' strategy sessions in Carrie's room, impressing them all with his passion for their fight.

Joe Hanover didn't have Confederate pedigree. He wasn't a born Tennessean. He was an immigrant. America had become his adopted home after he and his parents escaped the pogroms against Jews in their native Poland. His parents had taught him that America stood for justice, fairness, and equality. That was the American dream—and he believed in that dream. But it wasn't right that women didn't have equality as full citizens, he'd always felt. Now he had a chance to do something about it.

"The people of Tennessee have already passed upon suffrage!" he declared. "The real voice of the people has already been heard in the expression of both party platforms." Joe swiveled to face Seth Walker. "My colleagues

Mr. Bond and Mr. Walker were both members of the Democratic state convention in June which wrote into its platform that 'we stand for woman suffrage in Tennessee,'" Joe exclaimed.

Finally, *someone* was pointing out Seth's hypocrisy! Suffragists throughout the chamber burst into applause.

L. D. Miller stood again and moved to table Bond's delay resolution, to get rid of it for good.

Here was the first showdown, the first test of strength for both sides. The chamber was about to take a vote to shoot down the mass-meeting proposal. If the Anti legislators could kill the tabling motion, it would show they had the votes to delay, maybe even destroy, ratification.

The galleries, which had been electrified by the debate, now grew still. The roll call began.

"Mr. Anderson," the clerk called out. "Aye" was the first response, in support of tabling the resolution. The Suffs murmured approvingly.

"Bell"—aye; "Bond" and "Boyer"—no. The Antis were pleased.

Anita Pollitzer quickly tallied the votes. Men who'd pledged to support ratification, like Harry Burn, were now throwing their support behind the resolution to delay! Their pledges, their word, had been worth nothing. Catherine Kenny was keeping a similar tally for NAWSA. She noted, more optimistically, that four Anti delegates had now voted with the Suffs.

The clerk moved down the roll: "Riddick"—aye. "Turner"—no. And finally: "Speaker Walker"—no.

The Suffs did not have to wait for the clerk to announce his count; the delay resolution was dead. This was fantastic news! The Suffs cheered. The Anti spectators pursed their lips in silence.

Speaker Walker banged his gavel angrily and adjourned. That resolution hadn't gone according to plan at all, he thought as he stormed out of the statehouse. He needed time to think.

By late afternoon on Wednesday, the Hotel Hermitage was a hive of commotion. Men and women, Suffs and Antis, Democrats and Republicans all held meetings. Little cliques huddled in private, hatching plans. Suffs congratulated themselves on their victory while Antis dismissed the events of the day as no big deal. They still had time to flex their strength, Charlotte and Josephine assured each other confidently. In the lobby, Laura Clay and Kate Gordon handed out Anti literature spiked with racist and sexist malice. When they passed their former suffrage colleagues in the hallways, they looked the other way.

The legislators were really under pressure. Pressure from their party chiefs, from the governor, from the people of Tennessee. Adding to all this, both Suff and Anti advocates were chasing them down and pestering them with questions.

Often the women returned from their assignments frustrated. Both Suffs and Antis would try to find their delegates, only to realize that the men had been avoiding them.

On Wednesday evening, house member Tom Riddick and senate Speaker Andrew Todd made an important announcement. Both the house and the senate would vote on ratification on Friday, they declared. The votes appeared to be there, so why wait?

On one hand, it would be a relief to not delay the vote any longer. But those who were keeping careful count, like Sue White, recognized that things weren't *quite* so rosy. Sure, the Suffs had had just enough votes to defeat the *delay resolution*. But they had the bare minimum—fifty votes— needed to win the majority in the house. And in order to ratify, they needed a majority. There wasn't a single vote to spare.

It was another late night into dawn for the Nashville

soldiers. Once the Friday vote had been announced, they knew there'd be no time for sleep. The Antis and the Suffs knew they'd have to scramble to nail down the votes they needed within the next thirty-six hours.

As if that wasn't enough to worry about, the public hearing—a showdown debate between the Suffs and the Antis—was taking place that evening.

It was the hottest ticket in town.

That night, legislators, judges, and dignitaries jammed the house floor for the public hearing and debate. Suffs and Antis crowded onto the rose-bedecked balcony, squeezing by one another with pointed glances. Hundreds more people stuffed into the aisles and out the door. Governor Roberts settled into a seat near the front. The scene was as rowdy as a sports game. Fireworks were expected.

Initially, only men had been slated to speak, but Charlotte Rowe had demanded a speaking spot for the Antis. Native Tennessean Charl Williams, a Memphis educator and the vice chair of the Democratic National Committee, would represent the Suffs.

With ninety minutes for each side to make its case, the debate began.

U.S. Senator Kenneth McKellar on the Suffs' side urged Democrats to follow their party leaders—President Wilson and Governor Cox—to ratify.

Back and forth, men rolled out their arguments for and against the amendment. The Suffs waited anxiously as Charl Williams approached the podium. "The eyes of the United States are upon Tennessee." Charl's melodious voice rang through the chamber. "The women of the state and nation stretch out eager hands to our men in this fight."

Sue White winced slightly at this "damsel in distress" approach. If *she'd* been given a chance to speak in front of the whole legislature, she wouldn't have been quite so polite. Sue knew very well that any member of the Woman's Party was considered far too radical to speak in front of the legislature. That's why she wasn't up there, much as she'd like to have been. Sue would have demanded that the men step it up and stick out their necks for women and girls around the country. Once and for all. They were tired of waiting around for their rights! But even though Sue didn't exactly adore Charl's polite pleading with the men, she applauded supportively.

Then Charlotte Rowe took the stage. *All* the Suffs in the chamber smirked.

"Suffrage leaders are working to destroy the states and enslave the American people," Rowe declared in her customary take-no-prisoners style. She then launched into a bitter tirade against Mrs. Carrie Catt and the Tennessee suffrage women. Though they were tempted to boo, the Suffs in the galleries stuck their tongues out at Rowe instead.

The debate went on and on, winding down only as the clock struck midnight.

Sleepy legislators wiped their eyes and dreamed of heading to bed. But it was wishful thinking. Late as it was, there was still work to be done, and a decision to be made. The senate and house constitutional committees, small groups made up of members of each chamber, both withdrew. They would discuss, privately, whether to recommend ratification of the suffrage amendment.

The next steps for the women of Tennessee—and the entire nation—were in the hands of a select group of powerful men.

The senate committee's decision came first. The committee would recommend ratification of the suffrage amendment to the senate in the morning, they confirmed.

All of the Suffs—from the NAWSA members to the Woman's Party members—exhaled with relief.

But to their distress, things didn't go as smoothly in the house committee session. Seth Walker forced the men to postpone consideration of the ratification resolution, delaying any vote—yet again—until the following week.

14 ★ PETTICOAT GOVERNMENT

*R*atification would come down to a few simple numbers.

In the senate, the Suffs needed only seventeen out of thirty-three senators to support the amendment. There, things were looking good.

But in the house, the Suffs faced a tougher battle. And no one could predict when the ratification resolution would finally make it to the floor. The vote count kept fluctuating—and trending downward.

On Friday morning, a throng of Suffs and Antis pushed through the doors of the senate gallery, scrambling to grab a good seat. They were in for quite a show.

Andrew Todd gaveled the senate to order. The crowd hushed and faced forward. A senator stood. In his hands was a crisp piece of paper with neatly typewritten words on it. Here, finally, was the majority report of the Constitutional Amendments Committee.

The senator cleared his throat and began. The committee "is of the opinion that the present Legislature has both a legal and moral right to ratify the proposed resolution," he reported. "National woman's suffrage by Federal amendment is at hand," the senators wrote, "it may be delayed, but it cannot be defeated; and we covet for Tennessee the signal honor of being the 36th and last state necessary to consummate this great reform."

Cheers from the balcony rang out. Suffs hugged, laughing and squeezing one another's hands.

Senator Ernest Haston, the Suffs' floor leader in the senate, rose to place the ratification resolution itself before the senate for passage. There was a rustle of movement as the chamber braced for the main attraction. Senator Herschel Candler took the floor.

Anita Pollitzer squinted at him from her spot in the gallery. She remembered Herschel Candler. He'd given her a firm, square *no* when she'd reached out to him about supporting suffrage. Whatever he was about to say now wasn't going to do the Cause any favors.

Herschel saw himself as a man of the law. Lately, though, he'd felt abandoned by his Republican Party. He

This 1917 poster was used in the New York State campaign for woman's suffrage. It symbolized that the time for progress—for women to win the right to vote—had finally come.

Carrie Chapman Catt was the president of the National American Woman Suffrage Association from 1900 to 1904, and then again from 1915 to 1947. She came to Nashville to lead the efforts to ratify the Nineteenth Amendment.

Sue Shelton White had grown impatient with the slow, polite approach toward winning the vote, so she joined the more rebellious National Woman's Party. She led its ratification campaign in Tennessee, her home state.

After learning how to use sensational protest techniques in Britain, Alice Paul returned home to the United States to establish the National Woman's Party and launch a more aggressive campaign to win the vote.

Anita Pollitzer, a twenty-five-year-old artist, was a national organizer for the Woman's Party. Here she tries to persuade a Tennessee politician to side with the amendment.

A busy group of volunteers organize their attack on woman's suffrage at Anti headquarters in the Hotel Hermitage. Josephine Pearson stands to the right.

Nina Pinckard, president of the Southern Women's Rejection League, poses alongside Josephine Pearson at Anti headquarters. Between the women sits an elderly Confederate veteran of the Civil War.

In early 1917, with America on the brink of war, Alice Paul's Woman's Party began picketing in front of the White House. The protesters were called unpatriotic, and hundreds of women were arrested, imprisoned, and mistreated.

After suffering a stroke, President Woodrow Wilson became disabled in 1919. His wife, Edith, took on many decision-making powers in the White House, yet she opposed women having the right to vote.

Harry T. Burn of Niota was the youngest member of the Tennessee General Assembly. He wore a red rose when he entered the house chamber to vote on ratification on the morning of Tuesday, August 18, 1920.

On Friday, August 13, 1920, the Tennessee senate voted to ratify the Nineteenth Amendment.

When news of Tennessee's ratification reached Alice Paul on August 18, she sewed the thirty-sixth star onto her ratification banner and unfurled it from the balcony of the National Woman's Party headquarters in Washington, D.C.

The Nineteenth Amendment was officially added to the U.S. Constitution on August 26. When Carrie Catt returned home to New York City, she was greeted by a joyous parade.

In Nashville's Centennial Park in 2016, a statue by Alan Le Quire celebrating Tennessee's role in securing the Nineteenth Amendment was revealed. It depicts the suffragists (from left to right) J. Frankie Pierce, Carrie Chapman Catt, Abby Crawford Milton, Anne Dallas Dudley, and Sue Shelton White.

was trying to prevent woman's suffrage from infecting the nation. Women and politics? They had no business mixing. And now, glancing around the chamber, he saw women lobbyists in the crowds, in the balconies. Women who should be at home. Instead, they were invading the senate. It sickened him.

This federal amendment for woman's suffrage will destroy politics as we know it! Herschel began, loudly addressing the chamber. He insisted they couldn't be dominated by those Suffs and their "petticoat politics. . . . If there is anything I despise, it is a man who is under petticoat government!"

By now, his voice had risen to a full-on yell. The Suffs in the audience hissed at him.

"You are being dictated to by an old woman down here at the Hermitage Hotel whose name is Catt. Mrs. Catt is nothing more than an anarchist," he continued with disgust. Now even some of his fellow senators were booing Herschel.

"They would drag the womanhood of Tennessee down to the level of the negro woman!" Protests rained on him from every corner of the chamber. He steadied himself to make his final point. "Within a very few years after this amendment has passed, you will find that Congress has legislated so as to compel we people of the South to give to the negro men and women their full rights at the ballot box," he warned in a shrill voice. "Then you will find many of your counties, now dominated by the Democrats and white people, sending up negro representatives to this house."

The chamber broke into a frenzy of gasps as he sat down. Even his colleagues and the Antis were embarrassed by Herschel's emotional outburst. The Tennessee Suffs were outraged.

Harry Burn was sitting toward the back. He listened and did not speak. He admired Herschel Candler—Harry thought he was an excellent lawyer and a judicious man. In fact, Harry was studying law under Herschel's guidance. A young, ambitious man like Harry couldn't find a better model or mentor than Herschel Candler. But Herschel's uncontrolled outburst was jarring. He was speaking *way* out of line. It made Harry feel uncomfortable. Even a little angry.

Speaker Andrew Todd tried to calm the room in a stern but soothing tone: "That is the most unfortunate speech that has ever been made upon the floor of the senate. . . . These slurs do not meet approval of the good women of Tennessee," Andrew said in rebuttal, though clearly meaning the *white* women.

After Herschel Candler's outburst, the men of the senate all competed for a chance to speak up and sound knowledgeable and convincing. For almost three hours, a steady parade of them took the floor. Some rehashed the old arguments against mixing women and politics. Others made the case to ratify. Most condemned Herschel Candler's bitter remarks.

John Houk, Republican senator from the Knoxville area, stood to make a ringing speech. "In all my life I have never heard a sound argument against giving woman the right to vote: a woman is a human being and so is entitled to a vote in the making of laws affecting her and her children." Speaker Todd rapped his gavel to quiet the loud cheering.

More senators stood to make heartfelt entreaties for ratification. "I am voting for ratification because suffrage is right and just, not just because it aids either party," declared Albert Hill, upon whom the Suffs knew they could rely. "I believe that with equal suffrage we will have a better country and better government."

Erastus Patton of Knoxville gave a rallying cry that brought all yellow-flowered spectators to their feet: "Let's make Tennessee the Perfect 36th!"

Lunchtime came and went. Stomachs grumbled throughout the chamber. But the senators still had work to do.

Their time to vote on the ratification resolution had finally arrived. The Suffs squeezed one another's hands anxiously. Would they have enough men to carry through the amendment?

NO!

The roll call moved swiftly. An electric tension vibrated through the chamber. Before the Suffs knew it, the "aye" votes were climbing toward seventeen. Senator John Houk's "aye" was number fourteen on Sue White's tally sheet. "Aye" numbers fifteen and sixteen rolled in next. The clamor in the galleries grew louder. Everyone wearing yellow was up on their feet.

Aye!

"Matthews," the clerk called out.

"Aye," replied Matthews, and as the seventeenth vote in favor was cast, the gallery exploded in cheers and cries, waving of yellow banners, and deafening applause.

Speaker Todd banged his gavel repeatedly, but the Suffs didn't care. They knew they'd won the senate! They were halfway there, with just the house vote left.

All the way from the Hotel Hermitage, Carrie Catt and Harriet Upton could hear the cheers drifting up toward their windows.

15 ★ A CONSPIRACY

*T*hat weekend, newspapers across the country spread the word: the Tennessee Senate had voted *yes* to woman's suffrage.

The Suffs had really needed the confidence boost. Especially because the house still hadn't scheduled its vote on the amendment.

Antis tried to appear unfazed by the Suffs' senate victory. *Big deal!* Charlotte Rowe told the press. The senate vote was no indicator of suffrage's strength. The Antis were setting their sights on the house, where they were sure the amendment would be defeated. But while the Antis may have tried to *appear* cool and calm, behind the scenes their strategy meetings were frantic.

The Suffs held their own frenzied meetings, with Joe Hanover taking charge of strategy in the statehouse. Rumors continued to fly around. Apparently, some legislators were having second, and third, thoughts. And Major Edward Stahlman, the newspaper tycoon who'd promised Carrie Catt he had her back, had now switched to the Anti side. Carrie had suspected there was something shady about him. After all, his newspaper, the *Banner,* had published Nina Pinckard's cruel letter about Carrie only moments after Stahlman had declared himself pro-Suff. Now the *Banner* was going further, publishing a whole *flurry* of articles tarnishing the Suffs' names. *So the railroads have gotten to Stahlman, too,* Carrie said to Harriet, jabbing her finger at the latest issue of the *Banner.*

The Suffs had to stay focused. Their strategy was clear: once again, they had to find their delegates and convince them to stay on their side. They took their responsibilities seriously, inviting legislators to lunch and dinner, for a ride in the country, or for a game of cards. Anything to keep them out of the clutches of Anti workers. Or corporate lobbyists.

Finding these legislators wasn't so simple. All of them were tired and grumpy. Many had packed their bags to head home for the weekend. It made the Suffs very nervous to think of the lawmakers moving entirely outside of their grasp.

★ ★ ★

At the White House, Woodrow Wilson was feeling chipper. He spent his days sitting in his wheelchair, reading the paper in the sun of the portico. He worked for as many hours as his health allowed.

August was a humid month in Washington, D.C., and Wilson fanned his face with the paper to cool down. His first order of business for the day was to catch up on the ratification situation in Tennessee.

Ratification in that state was halfway there, Wilson's secretary reported to him. National woman's suffrage was almost clinched. For Woodrow Wilson, that meant one thing: thanks to all these new women votes, his League of Nations ideas would possibly become a reality—and he could take credit for a historic achievement.

But there was a hitch, Wilson soon learned: the Democratic Speaker of the Tennessee house, Seth Walker, was standing in the way of ratification. Walker was preventing the vote from even reaching the house floor!

At this, the president furrowed his brow. What could he do to help out the Suffs, he wondered. On Friday evening, he decided to send a telegram to Seth Walker, expressing "the earnest hope that the house over which you preside will concur in the suffrage amendment."

When the message reached Seth Walker in Nashville, he didn't take well to it. He answered the president's plea the next day. His tone was abrupt, even arrogant: "I have the profound honor to acknowledge your wire of Aug 13," Walker wrote. "[But] I do not believe that men of Tennessee will surrender honest convictions for political expediency or harmony." Apparently, even the president of the United States of America couldn't persuade him.

Carrie Catt was feeling under attack. Between the Anti women's nasty rumor-spreading, Nina Pinckard's slanderous opinion piece about her, and now Senator Herschel Candler's rant, Carrie may as well have been a punching bag.

On top of that, she was being flooded with anonymous letters, letters that were "vulgar, ignorant, insane," as she characterized them. They lashed out at her personally and said disgusting things about all suffragists. Carrie was also convinced that her phone was being tapped at the hotel.

Harriet Upton started noticing a man hanging outside Carrie's room, leaning with his ear to the door. It was obvious that he was listening in. *Ex*-cuse *me*, Harriet would bark, and he would scamper away. Other Suffs also noticed men loitering in the hallways near their rooms.

The Antis suspected that the Suffs were playing dirty tricks, too. Newspapers that held an Anti point of view, like the *Chattanooga Times* and now Edward Stahlman's *Banner*, were suddenly hard to find at Nashville newsstands. The Antis accused the Suffs of buying bundles of papers from delivery trucks, then destroying each issue before it could reach the hands of readers.

The Antis knew that the looming confrontation in the house was possibly their last stand. They were starting to get more aggressive—even physical. Harriet Upton was jostled in the Hermitage elevator by a group of Tennessee Anti women. They also shouted vile anti-Semitic slurs at Joe Hanover as he passed through the Hermitage lobby. It was getting nasty.

So *what* if the senate ratified the suffrage amendment? Josephine huffed to herself. She and the Antis were going to swing the house delegates against ratification—no matter what it took. They sniffed out any delegate who seemed noncommittal, uncertain, or open to having his mind changed. If he remained in Nashville over the weekend, they accidentally-on-purpose ran into him. If he was at home, they showed up at his door.

If sweet-talking didn't lead a man to their side, there were other ways to convince him that it was in his interest to vote against ratification. The Antis had a backup plan: bribery. Railroad men were swarming Tennessee, dangling lucrative jobs over the delegates' noses. Edward Stahlman could be seen circulating through the Hermitage, hard at work on legislators who'd pledged to ratify but now might be convinced to change sides. There were rumors of sacks of money being shipped into Nashville, too. Joe Hanover heard that Antis were even paying house members to not vote at all.

Enthusiasm for ratification was cooling, reporters noted. The excitement after the senate win was running low. And those smooth-talking corporate men in the Hermitage lobby—the railroad men, the textile factory and liquor lobbyists—were the main reason, pro-Suff Senator John Houk believed. And the Suffs simply didn't have the same kind of corporate support—or cash—that the Antis did.

On Sunday evening, Senator Houk set off alarm bells: "I believe one of the most powerful lobbies in the history of the Tennessee legislature is now at work to defeat ratification," he announced to reporters, "and if ratification is defeated the special interests of the state will be responsible."

Sue White knew just what John Houk was talking about: her latest polling numbers were slipping—again. Men who'd pledged for ratification were now hesitating. It was the Louisville and Nashville Railroad at work. She was convinced of it. The L&N had influenced the Tennessee legislature and politicians for generations. Powerful men like Edward Stahlman and Seth Walker were pushing the company's position against ratification—and the delegates were too intimidated to say no. There was no doubt anymore that Betty Gram had been onto something when she'd accused Seth Walker of cozying up to railroad interests just a few days before.

No man would be allowed to double-cross Sue White without a fight. Sue threatened to reveal the name of any delegate trying to wriggle out of his promise to vote for ratification. She'd show them for the hypocrites they were, she insisted.

By Sunday evening, August 15, the situation in the house seemed murkier than ever. After another long day of strategizing, Carrie Catt sat down at the writing desk in her hotel room. Wearily she pulled out a pen and paper. She needed to vent—but outside the hearing range of all those eavesdropping men and reporters. The best way to do it was to jot all her thoughts down. So she wrote a letter to a friend in New York, summing up the situation in Nashville:

We now have 35 ½ states. We are up to our last half of a state. With all the political pressure, it ought to be easy, but the opposition of every sort is here fighting with no scruple, desperately. Women, including L. Clay and K. Gordon, are here appealing to Negro phobia and every other cave man's prejudice.

Men, lots of them, are here. What do they represent? God only knows. We believe they are buying votes. We have a poll of the House showing victory but they are trying to keep them at home, to break a quorum and God only knows the outcome. We are terribly worried and so is the other side.

16 ★ ARMAGEDDON

*O*n Monday morning, the mood in Nashville was explosive.

The Hotel Hermitage looked like a battlefield. Men and women glared at each other suspiciously, flinging insults like confetti. The hotel—with its fancy lobby, its chandeliered dining rooms, its sunny verandas—had once been the perfect quiet place for afternoon tea, cake, and gossip. Now it was the scene of shouting matches, shoving, even fistfights.

At the start of the special session, the Suffs had sixty-two signed pledges for ratification from house members. The Antis said some of those men had pledged to them, too. Both sides tried to look relaxed. Both sides predicted victory. But everyone felt a cloud of uncertainty was hanging over the city of Nashville.

The newspaper headlines called it "Suffrage Armageddon."

★ ★ ★

Governor Albert Roberts hadn't gotten much sleep the night before. It wasn't just nerves keeping him up. He'd had a few surprise visitors come knocking at his door. A powerful group of newspaper publishers had shown up with a warning: Unless he changed his mind about ratifying, his political career was over. Edward Stahlman's *Banner* and other papers would all turn their editorial pages against him in the November election. Albert swallowed hard. Losing the next election was his greatest fear.

Joe Hanover had also been awakened that night. Threatening phone calls kept interrupting his sleep. The voices on the line were gruff and menacing: if he knew what was good for his health, they said, he'd back off from ratification.

More pro-Suff legislators received similar messages. Strange, anonymous voices called them late at night, threatening them if they didn't drop the suffrage cause.

If these sneaky techniques didn't work, the Antis had another trick up their sleeve. Perhaps suffrage-supporting legislators could be stopped from voting altogether. Legislators started getting phony telegrams claiming their wives were ill, their children were injured, their houses were on fire. Anything to get them to flee Nashville.

The Suffs could see right through these phony messages. They made it their duty to see that as many men as possible would make roll call.

That evening, hundreds of people gathered in the Hermitage lobby. The hallways and public rooms were packed with ladies in hats and men in summer suits. Everyone was in suspense. They were waiting for the House Committee on Constitutional Affairs and Amendments—a group of eighteen delegates, including Seth Walker and Joe Hanover—to finish their private meeting. The men were to come to a final decision: Would they recommend the ratification vote to the house or not?

Finally, after what felt like an eternity, the men emerged to reveal their final decision: the house would finally vote on ratification.

On the surface, this *seemed* like a good thing. But the Suffs knew they had good reason to worry.

Clearly, Seth Walker had a strategy. The quicker he could herd his Anti-supporting men to a full house vote, the better. The Antis were poised to beat the Suffs by just a few votes. So it made sense that he would agree to vote on ratification—only for the sake of voting no.

When Seth Walker strode out of the committee meeting, he told reporters: "We've got 'em whipped to a frazzle. We have ratification beaten, that is all there is to it."

As the house convened the next morning, the floor and galleries were once again crowded with red- and yellow-rosed men and women. This was the day of the vote. The halls were buzzing with urgent whispers, last-minute scheming, and latecomers trying to squeeze in before the proceedings began. Suff and Anti women fought over the seats and benches, elbowing one another for a standing-room spot. Squads of Suff decorators had been busy since dawn, tacking up bunting and banners, hanging flags. Some daredevil suffragist had even hung a big yellow sunflower above the Speaker's chair.

Waves of people surged toward the statehouse. A car filled with women factory workers had just pulled up in front; they were wearing red roses their boss had handed out—they'd been given the day off to swell the Anti ranks. Women who'd been in the suffrage fight for years came to watch history unfold before their eyes. Mothers brought their daughters.

Josephine Pearson settled into her seat and smoothed out her dress. She wanted to look her best for this historic occasion. That morning she had pinned three fresh red roses over her heart before leaving the hotel. These past weeks had been so exciting for her. The anti-ratification effort had been a huge success. And now it all came down to the statehouse. She was confident that the men of Tennessee would do their part to defend their white, southern heritage.

At half past ten, Seth Walker, his eyes swollen from lack of sleep, approached the Speaker's stand. He rapped his gavel firmly. The roll was called.

Tom Riddick kicked off the debate of the day. He put his dramatic skills to good use and opened with a bang—and a threat to the Antis:

"I have here the pledges of 62 members of this House to ratify the 19th Amendment, right here in black and white," he announced, "which the people of Tennessee will have the opportunity to read." A few legislators looked queasy. "You speak of your conscience?" Tom demanded. "What about your conscientious objections to violating your pledge?" More cheers from the yellow-rosed men and women. Flushed and quivering, Tom sat down.

For the next three and a half hours, the friends and enemies of ratification addressed the house. Almost every pro- and anti-suffrage argument ever voiced over the past seventy years came up.

Each time a speaker made a good point, fans cheered, whistled, and stomped. Others booed. Nice manners were a thing of the past. Each speaker was trying to outdo the other to win the crowd's approval.

Creed Boyer, an elderly Republican, went for a folksy approach: "Women are the best thing God ever made, and I honor women above all humankind. But I would not pollute them by allowing them to wade through the filthy waters of politics."

Catherine Kenny grimaced from her seat. She remembered Boyer. He'd pledged to ratify "until the cows come home." Now he was voting Anti! The Suffs' boos were drowned out by the Antis' applause.

"Taxation without representation should no longer apply to the women of the United States," cried a speaker for the Suffs.

"I would be ashamed to admit that my wife, my mother, or my sisters were not as capable of exercising the ballot as I am."

"The so-called elevation of woman in politics means instead her degradation."

"Tennessee must place the capstone on the temple of justice by becoming the 36th state."

The parade of speakers went on and on, hour after hour. The delegates got fidgety. The Suffs noticed and kicked into action; they'd already brought sandwiches and iced tea to feed the hungry legislators. It was a scheme to keep them from adjourning so that they could stay in the chamber longer for a vote. But security guards refused to let the Suffs distribute the food. Sandwiches sat uneaten. Hungry legislators grew grouchier.

Sue, Betty, and Anita stood together at the rear of the chamber. They were paying close attention to the delegates: who was listening, who was doodling, who was whispering to whom. Murmuring to one another, they kept note of the men they could trust—and especially the ones they couldn't. For example, the infuriating Harry Burn, who was annoyingly wearing a red rosebud in his lapel this morning. They'd really expected more from him. He seemed willing to tell each side what they wanted to hear. Recently he'd declared himself "undecided." But now here he was, voting against them!

Anita couldn't help noticing that Harry looked a little down, his face lined with worry. She almost felt sorry for him. He was her age, and awfully cute. He wasn't a smooth politician—he had a sweet, goofy awkwardness about him.

"I cannot pledge myself," he'd whispered to her and Betty when they'd last confronted him. "But I will do nothing to hurt you." What on earth did that mean? All they knew was that they couldn't trust Harry Burn.

After more than two hours of bitter back-and-forth, tempers heating up and stomachs rumbling, it was Seth Walker's turn to claim the floor. The chamber hushed as he approached the podium and launched into his speech.

Once again, he complained of the threat to Tennessee's states' rights and the "threat" of giving the vote to black women. "I am a Southerner from the bottom of my foot to the crown of my head! . . . We want this to remain a white man's country!" he shouted. The applause from the red-rosed crowds was deafening. Suffs caught each other's eyes and shook their heads in disgust.

Just then, Seth Walker pulled out a sheet of paper from his pocket. It was the telegram President Woodrow Wilson had sent him, pushing for ratification. At the mention of the president, the galleries exploded again, but now it was the Suffs causing a ruckus. Carrie Catt's close ally Anne Dudley climbed onto a bench behind the railing, where spectators were allowed to stand. "Wilson! Wilson! Wilson!" she cheered. Suffs echoed Anne's cry with whoops, whistles, and foot stomps. They went on for minutes, drowning out Walker's voice.

Seth paused, waiting impatiently for the rumpus to quiet. Finally, he read aloud his defiant reply to President Wilson. This time it was the Antis cheering rowdily.

But Seth Walker wasn't done. He still had his reputation to look after. "I have been insulted right here in this city. It has been said that the Louisville and Nashville Railroad had something to do with dictating my attitude," Seth added, brushing away the bribery claims. Anyone in the chamber who was paying close attention would have noticed that he never actually *denied* them, though.

Seth had spoken for almost an hour, mesmerizing the Antis with his passion and fury. As he finished his speech, he cried, "In good faith and good morals, we cannot ratify!"

It was Joe Hanover's turn now. The pressure was on.

"Women from the East, West, North, and South are looking to us to give them political freedom," Joe began. Suffs in the gallery nodded. "The entire world today has cast its eyes on Tennessee. This is a moral question, and that's why I am here, voting for this amendment." Applause.

Joe wanted to make a soaring oration for suffrage, but he couldn't allow Seth Walker's speech to go unchallenged. He wanted to tackle Seth head-on. Allowing his voice to rise, Joe said, "Certain interests have sent their lobbyists to ask members of this legislature to violate their pledges!"

Suffs in the galleries rained down boos. "And their agents are down at the Hermitage Hotel right now!"

Joe peered at the crowd for a moment. He appreciated the Suffs' enthusiasm. Overall, though, he could tell his colleagues had grown bored. It wasn't his fault, he knew. They'd been cooped up for hours. Stomachs ached with hunger. He figured he'd better rush to finish.

Only when we have given votes to the women of America, he concluded, *will our great state truly be a democracy.*

Cheers rang out for Joe. But before he could even get back to his seat, Seth Walker leapt up. "I move this House adjourn until tomorrow morning," Seth announced. The delegates would need more time to consider such a momentous decision.

Chaos broke over the chamber.

"No, no!" shouted Tom Riddick and Joe. "No, no!" Suffs echoed from the gallery. Further delay would play right into the Antis' hands! It gave them more time for bribes, more time to intimidate men into voting Anti. Yes, waiting any longer would be disastrous for the Suffs. They needed to vote—today.

But Seth rapped his gavel over the protests. The house was adjourned. Josephine Pearson and her comrades were all smiles as they bustled their way outside. Sue, Betty, and

Anita were silent and stunned. The hundreds of spectators still standing in the hallways looked confused.

Seth Walker couldn't help chuckling to himself as he headed back to his office. The move to adjourn was a fantastic play, he thought proudly. He'd outmaneuvered the Suffs. At least for now. But if he was honest with himself, he was also dreading the vote. Putting it off might give him time to bring a few more men to his side.

The NAWSA suffragists gathered for a meeting in Carrie Catt's room. The mood was bleak. Tearfully the women confessed their worries to one another. Even Carrie couldn't muster her usual optimistic pep.

Firmly, she gave her orders: Find your delegates. Keep them in your sight. Take them to dinner. Take them for a walk or a drive. Guard the platforms at Union Station, so no cowardly delegate can leave town before the vote. Be prepared for another night without sleep.

The latest polls looked terrible, Carrie knew. The count predicted ratification to fall short by two votes. The amendment, the Cause, and her whole life's work just might fall short and fail.

17 ★ THE HOUR HAS COME

*H*ousewives left the breakfast dishes in the sink. Clerks called in sick to work. Farmers gave the cows an early milking, then hopped into their trucks for the bumpy ride to the city. Whole families arrived, carrying picnic baskets.

On Wednesday morning, August 18, the citizens of Nashville and Davidson County came to the statehouse. They were hoping to see a historic moment firsthand. They arrived early, while the limestone statehouse glowed pink in the morning sun and the air was still blessedly cool. They perched themselves on the outdoor porticoes and spread out on the sloping lawns. From Carrie Catt's window, the scene looked like a giant carnival.

The Hotel Hermitage was no carnival, though. Certainly not on the floors where the Suffs were staying. Carrie and her comrades had barely slept. They were edgy and sad. The amendment didn't have enough votes to win ratification, and they knew it.

Nevertheless, they put on their white dresses and their yellow sashes. Sue and Betty attached their prison pins. Anita stuck a fresh yellow flower onto the brim of her hat. They found their assigned legislators and brought them to the capitol. Dozens of other suffragists were doing the same, masking their anxiety with bright smiles.

Meanwhile, the legislators were sick of being badgered by women and their party leaders. They were cranky. They wanted to go home. No matter which way the vote went, they hoped it would go quickly.

Governor Albert Roberts steered clear of the crowds that morning. Instead, he hung back in his office. He needed to catch up with his lieutenants before today's session began. He'd already dodged a couple of nervous phone calls from James Cox, who wouldn't leave him alone. The presidential candidate was demanding that Albert push the amendment through. As if it were all up to him! Albert didn't have a clue what to tell Cox. Things weren't looking good. And now Cox was calling again.

It's simple, Cox barked into Albert's ear: *If Tennessee*

ratifies, women will vote Democratic. They'll vote for me. They'll vote for you. We need them on our side. Now get it done, he warned before hanging up.

Albert clicked his phone back into place and groaned in frustration. That moment, he spotted Banks Turner, a young legislator, passing by his office. Banks, a thirty-year-old farmer from West Tennessee, had sided with the Antis on every vote. Albert had tried for weeks to convince him to switch, with no success. Banks Turner was stubborn as a mule.

The governor gave it one more shot.

Please, Banks, Albert pleaded with him, a burning look in his eyes. *Think about the long view. Suffrage will be good for Tennessee—for America!*

The young man didn't reply.

Banks, I'm asking you! Don't listen to what Seth Walker and his cronies are saying. We need to pass this amendment. There'll be trouble if we don't. Understand? Albert was frantic. His face was seized by panic as he waited for Banks Turner to say something, anything.

Banks looked at Albert thoughtfully. Then he looked away. He gathered himself up and walked away without another word.

Albert sighed despairingly. The time had come. He had no choice but to gear himself up for the day ahead. It was time to enter the chamber.

★ ★ ★

For decades, the suffrage fight—if reported at all—had been squeezed onto the "women's page" of newspapers, right next to the recipes and the housecleaning tips. Now the battle for the thirty-sixth state was being treated as breaking news. Front-page news, even. The kind of story that could rock the nation. There was no doubt: this was a big deal. The front of the house chamber was jammed with reporters.

Joe Hanover circled the room, shaking hands and patting backs. Anita Pollitzer and Betty Gram watched through narrowed eyes as the delegates trudged down the corridor and into the chamber. Harry Burn was on his way in, too, again wearing a red rose. "We really trusted you, Mr. Burn," they hissed at him, "when you said that you would never hurt us."

He turned toward them. "I mean that," he mumbled, making his way to his place in the third row.

Just then, a messenger brought an envelope to Harry's desk.

Speaker Seth Walker banged his gavel and brought the house to order at ten thirty-five a.m. The debate on the motion to ratify the amendment—the very last chance for

Tennessee to nail down the vote for women—could finally begin.

Speeches droned on for most of an hour, and the chamber seemed to slip into a stupor. The day was growing warmer, and heat seeped into the assembly hall. Women in the galleries fanned themselves with quick flicks of the wrist. Joe Hanover jumped from one man to another, whispering into their ears.

L. D. Miller demanded that the legislators free themselves from the grip of special interest lobbies. These lobbies had controlled the state legislature for years, he cried. It was time to start doing what was right for *people,* not for businesses!

The Suffs applauded enthusiastically.

Meanwhile, Harry Burn, over in desk forty-four, read the letter that had been delivered to him. Quietly he refolded it, pushed it back into its envelope, and tucked it into his pocket.

Up in the Speaker's chair, Seth Walker had done the calculations; he knew he had the votes he needed. He stepped down onto the floor. He looked a little too smug for the Suffs' comfort. They held their breath.

"The hour has come," Seth shouted with a melodramatic flair. "The battle has been fought and it is won. The measure is defeated." Some Suffs in the gallery began to sob. "I move that this measure goes where it rightfully belongs—to the table!"

The chamber exploded in shouts and cries. Tabling would kill the ratification resolution, knock it out of consideration. Joe Hanover and other Suff delegates jumped into the aisles, clamoring to be heard.

A chorus of Anti delegates yelled, "Second the motion!" from their desks. A suffragist in the gallery blew a siren horn in protest, adding to the ruckus.

Bang, bang, bang went the gavel, barely audible over the noise. Several chaotic minutes passed before a roll call could begin. Then the chamber quickly grew still.

By all counts, the Antis had the votes to defeat the amendment. They had forty-nine firm votes, the Suffs just forty-seven. The suffragists knew this was most likely the death of ratification in Nashville—and the United States of America.

The vote seesawed as the roll call progressed. The first set of names rejecting the tabling motion pleased the Suffs ("Anderson"—no; "Bell"—no). But the next set (Bond, Boyd, Boyer, Bratton, Burn), all voting "aye," sent them into despair. Anita Pollitzer crossed off Harry Burn's name with a grimace.

The Antis began to clap and cheer for every vote cast their way. The Suffs tried to keep pace. Back and forth it went, like a tennis game. But Seth Walker and Joe Hanover noticed one unexpected twist: Banks Turner, that stubborn young legislator who'd voted with the Antis all along, had actually just voted *not* to table. *That is an extra vote for the Suffs!* Joe realized.

The roll rushed on. The Antis seemed to own the end of the alphabet: "Weldon," "Whitfield," "Wilson," "Wolfenbarger," "Womack"—all voted aye. Women wearing yellow were weeping openly as Speaker Walker shouted the final "aye."

The Antis burst into a wild ovation. Their tallies showed the vote as 49 to 47 for tabling the amendment. *Victory!* they cried. The amendment was dead in Tennessee!

Hang on, everybody, calm down! the clerk shouted with a furrowed brow. He had a different count: his tally was tied, 48 to 48. A tie was *not* a majority—which meant that the motion to kill the suffrage amendment *hadn't* won.

The entire chamber erupted.

Delegates leapt from their chairs and rushed to the Speaker's stand, shouting. Seth Walker ran up the center aisle, fuming. That clerk was mistaken, he insisted.

The clerk sighed, warily agreeing to call a second vote.

The roll began again. "Anderson," "Bell"—no. "Bond," "Boyer," "Bratton," "Burn"—aye. On and on down the list. As the roll continued, Seth Walker walked down the aisle to the desk occupied by Banks Turner. Seth pulled up a chair and sat down beside him.

Banks had given a thumbs-down to ratification in every single meeting. What on earth was going on with him now? This was the final vote! Their last chance to destroy those Suffs!

Seth wrapped his arm around Turner's shoulder, whispering urgently into his ear. Suffs watched with alarm: Was Seth *threatening* the one delegate who might save the ratification resolution from doom?

The roll call headed toward the tail end of the alphabet, the Ss and the Ts. "Travis"—aye. "Tucker"—no. "Turner . . ." There was a pause. Everyone held their breath. Suddenly Banks Turner shook off Seth Walker's arm from his shoulders, bolted up from his chair, and declared: "Nay."

"The second ballot is tied, 48 to 48," the clerk reported, his voice firm. The Suffs shrieked joyfully before he could even finish his sentence. Seth stormed away from Turner's desk. *Fine,* he fumed to himself. The tabling motion was lost, but the larger battle could still be won.

Then, finally, the vote to ratify the Nineteenth Amendment was called. It all came down to this vote, this moment.

Joe Hanover felt like he'd been holding his breath for hours. Now he could finally exhale. Banks Turner had saved the day on that last vote. Still, there was no knowing whether Banks was going to stick with the Suffs on this next one. And even if he did, it might not do the trick. If the vote was tied, ratification would die. Joe needed *two* more solid votes. And he had no hope of finding them this late in the game.

The sun blazed as the clock struck noon. The clerk shuffled the papers on his desk. Roll call began once again. The tension in the chamber was painful. Josephine Pearson felt a surge of excitement. Abby Milton and Catherine Kenny glanced at each other nervously. There was nothing else they could do. The decision was out of their hands.

The clerk started from the top again, in a slow, careful voice. "Anderson . . . Bell . . ."

Then Harry Burn heard his name called. He knew most of his constituents didn't want woman's suffrage. Other politicians had warned him that, for the sake of his career, he'd best vote against it. He was torn. Personally, he favored giving women the vote. It was only fair and right. Then again, he also wanted to be reelected in the fall. He wanted a career. He was supporting his widowed mother, making extra cash as an agent for the local railroad. The railroad company was against the amendment, too.

Rejection really was the safest course. But now . . . with

Banks Turner possibly flipping, suddenly siding with the Suffs . . . there would be a tie. That meant ratification could hinge on a single vote. His. The sound of his name echoed in his ears.

In his jacket pocket sat the letter that had arrived earlier in the morning, written in a fine, very familiar hand: "Dear Son: Hurrah and vote for suffrage and don't keep them in doubt. . . . I've been waiting to see how you stood but have not seen anything yet. Don't forget to be a good boy and help Mrs. Catt. . . . With lots of love, Mama."

"Aye," said Harry Burn.

Sue White's pencil froze on her tally sheet. The clerk moved on to call the next person. Harry's reply was so unexpected, said so quickly, that few even noticed it. Then came a rumble of astonishment as it all sank in. Had *Harry T. Burn* just voted "aye" for ratification?

Suffs rose to their feet and roared, drowning out the clerk's voice. It took several minutes to regain order. Seth Walker and the Anti delegates drilled their eyes into Harry's back. They waved their hands in disgust. This fickle young man had betrayed them!

Anita Pollitzer and Betty Gram were overjoyed. "My vote will never hurt you," Harry had told them. He'd given them no good reason to actually believe him. But in the end, he was right—he'd possibly saved them.

Of course, Harry brought them to a tie. Only if Banks Turner stuck with them could they win. Everyone hushed, waiting in agony.

That's when they saw that Seth Walker was again whispering menacingly to Banks. The clerk called, "Tarrant"—aye. "Thronesbury"—no. "Travis"—no. "Tucker"—aye. "Turner . . ."

Silence. Banks Turner did not reply. "Mr. Turner," the clerk called again. Suffs bit their lips. Joe Hanover froze at his desk. Harry Burn swiveled his head to see Turner. "*Mr. Turner,*" the clerk called once more. Banks remained silent. The clerk marked Banks Turner as not voting.

Soft whimpering could be heard in the balconies.

The roll call spiraled toward its conclusion with the Ws, and the Antis leaned forward in happy anticipation as the clerk called: "Speaker Walker." Seth Walker shouted, "No." The final tally was 48 to 48. It was over. The amendment was defeated. Josephine Pearson, Charlotte Rowe, and Nina Pinckard were on their feet, ready to cheer. But before a single sound could leave their throats, Banks Turner abruptly stood up from his chair.

Banks was a thin young man with a serious face. Everyone could see the beads of sweat on his forehead. He took a quick breath, then spoke.

"Mr. Speaker," Banks called out, "I wish to be recorded as voting aye."

There was a moment of silence. Silence and shock. Then an explosion. A roar erupted, the likes of which was never before heard in that old statehouse. The chamber shook with screams and cries, with thumping and whooping. Anne Dudley's shriek pierced the chamber. Those who could dance in the jammed chamber did. Men and women wept. Joe Hanover was mobbed by delegates, like the winning pitcher of a ball game. Hundreds of tiny yellow flags and flower petals rained down from the balconies.

The clerk hadn't even announced the tally, but the Suffs didn't care. They could count. With Harry, and then Banks, it was 49 to 48.

While the Suffs celebrated, the Antis raged. They hurled insults and threats upon Harry Burn. *Traitor!* they cried. Through the uproar a loud voice rang out. It was Seth Walker's. "I wish to change my vote from nay to aye."

"And," Seth shouted over the din, "I wish to move for reconsideration." It was a very devious move! By changing his vote to the winning side, the Speaker of the house could demand a do-over anytime within the next two days.

But none of that mattered at this moment. The Suffs were too busy celebrating to pay attention to his shenanigans.

★ ★ ★

From her hotel window, Carrie Catt could hear the wild commotion. In her bones, she knew. They'd done it. Women with yellow flowers in their hair ran down the hill toward the Hermitage. They were coming to bring her the news she'd been waiting a lifetime to hear. Harriet Upton's heart pounded in her chest as she watched the Suffs cascade down the hill, laughing and crying with joy.

Alice Paul, waiting in Washington, received a rush wire from Nashville. Calmly she rose and went to her worktable. Then, with a full heart, she stitched a thirty-sixth star onto a cloth banner: a flag to represent each state that had passed ratification.

18 ★ LIBERTY BELL

The Suffs felt like they were walking on air. Their right to vote was finally in sight, and with it a chance to empower women and give hope to girls throughout the nation. But their joy was quickly brought down a notch. That sneaky Seth Walker's last play for reconsideration had put a giant question mark over ratifying. A second vote on ratification could overturn the first one—that is, unless they upheld the majority. They couldn't afford to lose a single vote.

Despite their anxiety, there must have been quite a joyous scene in Carrie's room at the Hermitage. Carrie couldn't stop grinning. Harriet Upton's mischievous laugh filled the room. Anne Dudley clasped hands with Catherine Kenny and Charl Williams.

Meanwhile, Sue White, Betty Gram, and Anita Pollitzer jumped for joy in the Nashville Woman's Party headquarters. Sue dictated a report to Alice Paul. She received a speedy reply: "Splendid Work. Hold the Fort." Sue felt a surge of pride. They'd done it! They just had to stay strong for two more days. It was going to be a very long forty-eight hours, she thought with a sigh.

While the Suffs understood that their work was not *quite* done, the rest of the world assumed the house vote was the final step for women's enfranchisement. Thousands of congratulations poured into Nashville.

"The civilization of the world is saved," exclaimed James Cox. Women voters, he assumed, would support the League of Nations, bringing on peace for generations. Better yet, he thought, women would vote for *him* to be the next president.

James Cox's opponent in the presidential election, Warren Harding, also issued a statement. "All along I have wished for the completion of ratification and have said so," he said, a bit defensively, "and I am glad to have all the citizenship of the United States take part in the presidential elections." The Suffs rolled their eyes at Harding's remarks. He'd barely stuck his neck out for them at all! He might as well have called himself an Anti.

Carrie, true to form, felt confident that the "hour of victory" had arrived. She issued a statement of fierce optimism and simple eloquence:

Our mothers began it. So it came on to us as, in a way, a sacred trust. And a great part of our rejoicing today in the hour of victory is compounded of our feeling of loyalty to the past and our satisfaction that we have stood faithful to its trust. . . . With a new purpose, the purpose of making the vote register for an improved citizenship, the women of the National [NAWSA] are already lined up under a new name, the League of Women Voters.

From Washington, D.C., Alice Paul had already given the press a prime photo opportunity: the unfurling of her ratification banner from the balcony of the Woman's Party headquarters. She gave reporters a statement, calling on women to persist in the name of true equality:

With the power to vote achieved, women still have before them the task of supplementing political equality with equality in other fields. . . . The vote will make it infinitely easier for them to end all discriminations and they will use the vote towards that end.

Alice could not possibly imagine just how long that task would take.

★ ★ ★

The first thing Harry Burn had done after escaping from the statehouse was to call his mother. Febb Burn was delighted to hear from her son. She was so proud that he'd taken her advice. His vote for ratification had put the whole thing through.

Phoebe (Febb) Ensminger Burn was a sharp-witted woman. She liked to keep up with current events. It was absolutely ridiculous that women couldn't vote, she'd always said. Why should women and girls have no say in what happened in the country? "I am for progress," she'd say, explaining her pro-suffrage attitude. It wasn't a popular opinion in rural Tennessee.

Febb had been keeping track of the special session in Nashville while Harry was away. She'd been disappointed to find no mention of her adored son in the local papers' reports. She was hoping and praying that Harry would support ratification. She knew he was under a lot of pressure about it. So she'd written a letter to him with that crucial maternal advice.

It had turned out to be *just* the thing the Suffs needed to change the course of ratification.

★ ★ ★

Governor Albert Roberts was in his office at the capitol, thanking the men who'd stuck with him through the vote. He'd turned out to be one of the most faithful, and courageous, woman's suffrage supporters in the statehouse. He couldn't have been more relieved that the ordeal was essentially over. Alice Paul wired him her personal thanks for his "splendid fight" for ratification. Even vice presidential nominee Franklin Roosevelt congratulated him: "The action of Tennessee assures the greatest step that could possibly be taken for human rights and better American citizenship."

But Albert also received other telegrams that were less positive, and more threatening, such as the one signed by more than a hundred men in Fayetteville: "Protect the rights of our states against federal encroachment. . . . Dissatisfaction that exists here will seriously endanger your election in November."

We'll destroy ratification in the next vote, the Anti leaders bragged. They sent hate mail and made bullying phone calls to every legislator who supported ratification—especially Banks Turner and Harry Burn. If they could scare just one legislator into switching to their side, they could still win. Anti-suffrage protests (they called them "indignation" rallies) sprang up around the state, filled with racist and sexist chants and speeches.

The Suffs knew they had to remain alert. Day and night

they guarded hotel halls and lobbies, Union Station, and taxi stands. Quite a few delegates were already grumbling that they wanted to go home, that they were tired and missed their families. But the Suffs wouldn't allow it. They needed every delegate to stay put and vote one last time.

The Antis, on the other hand, wanted to get rid of as many delegates as possible. Anything to sway the reconsideration vote in their favor. They were desperate, and they weren't afraid to stoop low. Fake telegrams calling delegates home for family emergencies kept popping up. The Antis planted a blackmail story, accusing Joe Hanover of paying off Harry Burn. Even kidnappings were rumored.

Everyone returned to the house chamber for the morning session: frazzled legislators, hopeful Suffs, testy Antis, anxious onlookers. Cheers and applause rang from the galleries as the delegates entered. Seth Walker, Joe Hanover, Banks Turner, and Harry Burn strode in. All of the Anti delegates were in attendance, as well as all the men who'd voted for ratification. The question was whether any of the Suff men had been persuaded to change their minds overnight.

After the banging of the gavel and the opening remarks, everyone noticed Harry Burn rise from his desk. Apprehensively, he asked to speak. The galleries buzzed. It was

Harry's chance to explain himself. To speak up for suffrage in his *own* words.

"I want to state that I changed my vote in favor of ratification first because I believe in full suffrage as a right; I believe we had a moral and legal right to ratify . . . [and] I appreciated the fact that an opportunity such as seldom comes to a mortal man to free seventeen million women from political slavery was mine," Harry declared. He paused, and with a slight, sly smile concluded: "And I knew that a mother's advice is always safest for a boy to follow, and my mother wanted me to vote for ratification." Flushed, Harry returned to his seat. His earnest, emotional statement made the Suffs proud. They smiled at him from the galleries and balconies.

The house adjourned until the next morning.

But before the Friday session convened, Joe Hanover faced another worrisome problem. Tom Dodson, a young East Tennessee lawyer who was an enthusiastic suffragist, needed to go home: his baby was extremely ill, possibly dying. And this wasn't some cruel Anti prank phone call. This was real. A heartbroken Dodson sprinted to catch the next train home to his family. He was already on his way to Union Station when Joe Hanover and the ratification leaders realized he was gone.

Tom Dodson's vote was *absolutely* needed to thwart Seth Walker's move to reconsider.

What could they do? the Suffs worried. That's when suffrage supporter Newell Sanders piped up. He offered to charter a special train to get Tom Dodson home—if Tom would stay for the pivotal vote. But they'd have to find Tom, and fast. So a group of Suffs dashed to the station, arriving just as Tom's train was blowing its departure whistle. The Suffs jumped onto the train, pleading with him to stay, and promising that the special express train would speed him home instantly. Once the vote was complete, that is. Tom hesitated for a moment. But he knew there was no time to spare. Moving quickly, he nodded, grabbed his bag, jumped off the train, and darted back to the capitol.

Joe Hanover sighed with relief when he saw Tom Dodson running back into the chamber. Tom's presence today would make all the difference in the world.

Now, as everyone hushed and took their seats, Seth Walker approached the Speaker's stand. There was no mistaking it: Seth looked haggard and pale. His expression was nervous. After Harry's speech yesterday, and with Tom Dodson back at the capitol, it was obvious that he hadn't managed to budge any of the forty-nine men who'd voted for suffrage. What he needed was more time.

Clearing his throat, he called a vote to delay the decision.

Surely if he managed to postpone the vote until Monday, he could bribe a few men to vote Anti by then.

For days, Seth Walker had been boasting that he had the votes to overturn ratification, once and for all. The Suffs weren't sure whether he was all bluster, but his threats scared them. They were so close to passing the amendment! It would be absolute agony to have it all fall through now. Throughout the capitol, everyone held their breaths.

Once again, each legislator's name was called.

Suff women squeezed each other's hands. Anti women pursed their lips. Joe Hanover's eyes darted from legislator to legislator as they called out their responses. Harry Burn sat back in his seat and bit his lip. Seth Walker found himself tapping his foot anxiously. Things weren't looking good for the Antis, and Seth knew it.

The Monday postponement was voted down, 49 to 47.

Sure enough, the suffrage line held firm.

There was a moment of barely contained silence. And then a burst of thunderous applause. Cheering could be heard echoing through the halls of the majestic capitol building. Suffs broke into song. A suffragist on the floor rang a mini version of the Liberty Bell. They had persisted—and they had come out on top. The time for Seth Walker's reconsideration

had run out. Tennessee's ratification of the suffrage amendment had *officially* been passed. It was finally done. American women had, at long last, won their right to vote.

Seth looked down at his shoes, crushed. Josephine Pearson and the Anti women in the galleries glared at him, disgusted.

Tears flowed down the Suffs' cheeks as they left the chamber. They stopped at Governor Roberts's office on the first floor and thanked him gleefully for his help. Out the doors and down the steps of the capitol they sang "My Country, 'Tis of Thee" over and over, their voices ringing especially loud during the phrase "sweet land of liberty."

"You are all heroes," Carrie Catt exclaimed to the legislators when she heard the news, "your names will forever be written on the hearts of American women."

"The victory is complete," Alice Paul crowed. "It is a victory for humanity."

The women of the United States had finally won the right to vote; girls could look forward to voting when they were older, and a new chapter of American history opened.

A devastated Josephine Pearson retired to her room "tired and heart-sick," as she described it. Losing the ratification fight "embarrassed my self-respect, and also lost something of trust, never quite restored," she confessed. She felt an emptiness, "a void," such as she had never experienced in her life.

The suffragists didn't have to wait long for their enemies to vow revenge. The Antis held rallies demonizing Governor Roberts, calling for his reelection defeat in November. Seth Walker, Charlotte Rowe, and Edward Stahlman spoke at rallies with "Save the South" themes. The tone was often racist, and these events were attended by numerous Ku Klux Klan members, who grew increasingly violent.

The Antis could kick and scream all they wanted. Carrie Catt couldn't have cared less. Tennessee had ratified. Woman's suffrage was now American law. *That* was what mattered. Carrie could finally pack her bags. On Wednesday, August 25, she, Harriet Upton, Marjorie Shuler, and Charl Williams left Nashville's Union Station.

The following day, in the early morning hours of August 26, the Nineteenth Amendment entered the Constitution of the United States.

The next afternoon, Carrie Catt went to the White House to personally speak to Woodrow Wilson. She thanked President Wilson for all his help in the ratification fight. But she sensed the bitter sadness in Wilson, even as he was congratulating her: she'd finished her fight for woman's suffrage, but he would likely never be able to finish his for the League of Nations.

And while suffragists were celebrating the beginnings of a new political era, an editorial writer for the *Baltimore Afro-American* newspaper offered his readers a chilling view of the situation:

> Woman's Suffrage is now a fact. Candidate Harding and candidate Cox importuned the Tennessee legislature to join in the ratification of the 19th Amendment, but it was not until after the [lawmakers] were assured that it would be as easy to disenfranchise Negro women as it has been to disenfranchise Negro men that they consented to lift the ban and permit the passage of the Suffrage measure. Under the "wide discretion" allowed the election officials in the state of Tennessee it has been a very easy matter to disqualify a male Negro applicant for certificate to vote. It will be just as easy to disqualify the female Negro applicant. And thus we take another step in the great work of making the world safe for democracy.

On Friday morning, August 27, Carrie Catt arrived home. When she reached New York's Pennsylvania Station, a band was playing. It took her a moment to realize the music was for *her.* Close friends, powerful politicians, and hundreds of Suffs were all there to greet her on the platform. They called her name, reached out to touch her, cried out congratulations. Carrie tried to say hello to everyone as best she could while swallowing back happy tears.

The New York City Suffs presented her with an enormous bouquet of flowers tied with a suffrage-yellow satin ribbon that read: "To Mrs. Carrie Chapman Catt from the Enfranchised Women of the United States."

A parade began in her honor. Carrie, Harriet Upton, and Charl Williams rode in an open limousine decked out in yellow and gold. Cheers sang out as they passed. Hundreds of parading women wore white dresses with yellow sashes and carried the banners of their suffrage societies. *If only Susan Anthony could be here to see this!* Carrie thought. The first generation of Suffs would have been so proud.

Thousands of spectators on the sidewalks cheered and clapped, and trumpets blared as Carrie Catt led the parade. Carrie's homecoming celebration was the happiest moment of her whole life.

Bells rang all across the country at noon on Saturday, August 28. Women's enfranchisement was official! The bells were Carrie Catt's idea. Church and school bells pealed, factory and train whistles blew, firehouse sirens blared, and car horns tooted. But the bells and whistles were quiet in Tennessee. Indignation rallies were raging across the state. The Antis were still bitter. But Anne Dudley, Catherine Kenny, and all of the other Tennessee Suffs didn't let that stop them. They celebrated proudly.

After an adrenaline-packed summer, Carrie Catt could finally settle back into her quiet home life. Sitting at her own desk, overlooking her garden, Carrie wrote an emotional note. It was dedicated to all the women and young girls of the nation:

> The vote is the emblem of your equality, women of America, the guaranty of your liberty. That vote of yours has cost millions of dollars and the lives of thousands of women. Women have suffered agony of soul which you never can comprehend, that you and your daughters might inherit political freedom. That vote has been costly. *Prize it!*
>
> The vote is a power, a weapon of offense and defense, a prayer. Use it intelligently, conscientiously, prayerfully. Progress is calling to you to make no pause. *Act!*

19 ★ ELECTION DAY

On November 2, 1920, American women did act—they voted.

In cities and towns, women headed to their local polling stations. They smiled and chatted together as they waited in line. Housewives voted on their way to the grocery store. Office and factory workers went over their lunch breaks. Rural women made their way to the polls through fierce snowstorms. Mothers brought their babies, carrying them in their arms.

Carrie Catt cast her ballot at the polling place near her Manhattan apartment. Alice Paul voted for the first time in her life nearby in New Jersey. The Tennessee Suffs voted in their districts. At Hyde Park, Eleanor Roosevelt also voted for the first time, probably for her husband and the Cox/FDR Democratic ticket.

On the morning of Election Day, Josephine Pearson

went to her polling site, but she wasn't planning on voting. She came to pass out pamphlets claiming the Nineteenth Amendment was illegal. The poll watchers were surprised to see her: *You're not voting?* they asked. She declined, but men at the polls came up with a solution: "Tell us what you want voted and we'll vote for you!" In every subsequent election, Josephine Pearson had a local man cast her ballot for her.

The ten million women who voted helped to elect Warren G. Harding in a landslide. The nation was weary. Money was tight for many Americans. People were frightened by dramatic newspaper headlines and by the threat of rising power in Russia. So, many of them embraced Harding's promise of "America First"—which meant a withdrawal from any international entanglements, including the League of Nations. Fearful that a white, Christian majority was being threatened by immigration, the new administration and Congress would soon close American borders to new immigrants.

Americans picked a conservative president who promised a "Return to Normalcy" after a disruptive war. They hoped to reclaim a sense of security after a difficult era. Unfortunately, Harding's character was weak, and his short term (he died of a heart attack in his third year in office) was defined by corruption and scandal.

Governor Albert Roberts lost his election that November. His effort to ratify the suffrage amendment didn't do him any favors at the polls. Angry Antis voted against him, instead checking off the name of Republican Alf Taylor. Carrie Catt was greatly disappointed to hear of Albert's loss. Suffrage's brave friends should be rewarded, not punished, she believed. She wrote him a personal letter of sympathy—and of gratitude.

Even so, Harry Burn was thriving. To the delight of the Woman's Party and NAWSA women, he was reelected to the Tennessee legislature by the citizens of Niota.

Overall, the voting turnout was disappointing to the suffragists. In the end, after all that struggle, only a third of eligible women cast ballots in the election.

People expected Carrie Catt to explain what had happened. It wasn't because of a lack of enthusiasm, she insisted. It was difficult to register to vote with so little time—only ten weeks—between ratification and the election. And some women who *wanted* to vote were prevented from doing so. To prevent black women from voting, Mississippi and Georgia refused to extend their registration deadlines.

But Carrie wasn't discouraged. She had her work cut out for her. Now that she'd helped secure the vote, her next order of business was to get as many women as possible out there and voting in the next election.

Carrie's group, the League of Women Voters (LWV), was up for the task. The league's goal was (and still is) to educate voters—men and women, immigrants and American-born citizens—of all ages. It informs women and girls on how to get involved in political issues and activism—on "making democracy work." The League of Women Voters is still active in all fifty states, after over a hundred years. Carrie Catt herself continued as the LWV's honorary president and national board member for the rest of her life.

The National Association for the Advancement of Colored People (NAACP) was established in 1909. Its mission is "to secure the political, educational, social, and economic equality of rights in order to eliminate race-based discrimination and ensure the health and well-being of all people."

On that same Election Day 1920, racist incidents unfolded across the country. In Boston, black women got fake notices warning them that they might face fines and prison if they registered to vote. Throughout the southern states, black women were intimidated and assaulted. State troops were on call to guard polling places. But the state troopers were all white—and failed to adequately protect black people who were attempting to vote. The

NAACP's request for federal troops to protect black voters from harassment was denied.

Nearly four thousand black women and men were denied their voting ballots in Jacksonville, Florida. The worst episode of violence was in Ocoee, Florida, near Orlando, where the Ku Klux Klan murdered as many as fifty black men and women who had attempted to vote. They lynched several men, and a woman burned to death as the white mob set fire to twenty-five homes and two churches in the black section of town.

After the election, NAACP officers testified before Congress and brought evidence of the violent suppression of black voters in the southern states. A veteran white suffragist, Mary Ovington, implored other suffragists to rise to the occasion: "We must not rest until we have freed the black as well as white of our sex," she implored. "Will you not show us how to make the 19th Amendment the democratic reality that it purports to be?" But many other white suffragists, satisfied that they finally had their own right to vote, ignored the plight of their black sisters.

To **suppress** is to forcefully prevent something from happening.

To this day, Congress has never used its powers to

punish states for voting rights violations. The United States government looked away as black voters were violently suppressed from voting for decades. It wasn't until the Voting Rights Act of 1965 that black citizens were given the legal tools to challenge the ways their constitutional right to vote had been violated.

But in 2013, the U.S. Supreme Court overturned the act's most effective enforcement tool: Section 5, which requires states with a history of racial discrimination to seek federal approval before making any changes to voting rules. Voter suppression throughout the United States—in the South, as well as in districts in other states with minority populations—remains a serious problem. In most states, access to the vote is taken away from people who have served time in prison, even after they are released.

Voting rights continue to be threatened in states across the country. There are restrictive registration requirements. Voter ID laws. Limitation on early voting opportunities. There are also inadequate polling place resources in neighborhoods whose populations are mostly people of color, specifically black, Latino, and Native American neighborhoods.

Although white women got the vote in 1920, other Americans were forced to wait. Native Americans weren't granted citizenship and suffrage until 1924—yet many

Native Americans were still banned from voting by state laws until the 1950s. Asian American women and men weren't permitted to become citizens or vote until the late 1940s. African Americans in southern states had suffrage on paper, but they weren't allowed to really freely vote until 1965. Many still face obstacles today.

After the fight for suffrage was won, the women of the movement set off in new directions. Carrie Catt led the women of NAWSA into its successor organization, the League of Women Voters, and into its mission of voter education and issue advocacy. Alice Paul's National Woman's Party kept going, with new ambitious goals. Winning suffrage was just the *first* step toward full equal rights for women. Women deserved equality in every part of their lives: in education, the workplace, and their professions. For Alice and her Woman's Party colleagues, the fight would go on.

Sue White stayed with the Woman's Party while she joined the staff of Tennessee senator Kenneth McKellar in Washington. She was able to achieve her dream of becoming a lawyer, earning her degree in 1923. With the help of Sue White, Alice Paul and Woman's Party activist Crystal Eastman drafted the Equal Rights Amendment— a constitutional amendment prohibiting discrimination on account of sex. The amendment was introduced into Congress in 1923. Almost one hundred years later, in January 2020, the ERA was ratified by a thirty-eighth state—Virginia—which meant it had reached the threshold for ratification. (The threshold is three-quarters of the states.) Although the deadline imposed by Congress for ratification had long since expired, there are questions about whether such a deadline is unconstitutional. It is likely that the future of the ERA, and its ratification, will be decided by the courts.

Following their loss in 1920, the Antis grew in power over the next decades. Immediately after ratification, Anti women switched to fighting against federal government programs for maternal and child welfare, an end to child labor, and public health programs. These programs, they asserted, were "radical" and Communist-inspired plots to secretly destroy the American family.

In the 1960s and 1970s, the "second wave" of feminism opened up to a new generation the national conversation about women's rights. Second-wave feminists demanded total equality. In the workplace. In their homes. In their classrooms. On the sports field. They demanded control of their own bodies, their own careers, and their own bank accounts. Many of these issues are still discussed today. After all, on average, working women *still* earn 20 percent less than working men. But there's been some definite progress. More women have entered the ranks of corporate executives, and half of medical and law school students are now female. In the most recent Congress, about 25 percent of representatives are women. So are three of the nine Supreme Court justices.

The suffragists' struggle has inspired other American social justice movements for over a century. Their lobbying and grassroots organizing, their nonviolent protests, their use of legal challenges—all these techniques influenced black civil rights campaigners, anti–Vietnam War protest groups, and AIDS and LGBTQ+ activists. The future will undoubtedly bring more causes to fight for, but the suffragists proved that passionate civic activism can triumph over outdated and unequal rules and laws.

Luckily, there's a strong legacy for us *all* to look to. The fight goes on.

On the ninety-sixth anniversary of the Nineteenth Amendment—August 26, 2016—more than four hundred people gathered in Nashville's Centennial Park. A small group of Tennessee women activists, calling themselves the Perfect 36 Society, had raised almost $1 million to commission a statue. It would be dedicated as the Tennessee Woman Suffrage Monument.

The bronze statue depicts five heroines of the Nashville ratification battle, striding confidently together. Four are Tennessee Suffs—Sue White, Anne Dudley, Abby Milton, and Frankie Pierce—and the fifth is Carrie Catt. They look like they're setting out on a march, moving forward proudly.

On the morning of the dedication, many women in the audience were dressed in classic suffrage costumes—long white dresses with yellow sashes and flowers. Everyone wore yellow rosebuds. Anne Dudley's grandson and great-grandchildren were there. So were the descendants of Governor Albert Roberts. Speakers gave emotional thanks to the suffrage pioneers.

When the statue was unveiled, crowds surged forward to admire and touch it. Mothers brought their daughters to stand at its feet. Here were the activists who'd fought in that last great battle for woman's suffrage. Smiling Tennesseans, black and white, posed for photos and selfies with their heroic foremothers.

Ten weeks later, on Election Day 2016, in celebration of the possibility that a woman might be elected president of the United States, thousands of women made an emotional pilgrimage: first to their polling place and then to a cemetery. They cast their ballots for Hillary Rodham Clinton, the first woman to run for president as the candidate of a major political party. Then they visited the graves of the suffrage leaders who'd won that ballot for them. In Rochester, New York, almost ten thousand women brought flowers and their "I VOTED" stickers to decorate Susan B. Anthony's headstone. In New York City's Woodlawn Cemetery, women voters decorated Elizabeth Cady Stanton's and Carrie Catt's graves. In New Jersey, Alice Paul's grave was showered with bouquets, stickers, and thank-you notes. And in Nashville, the new woman's suffrage monument in Centennial Park was covered with bouquets of yellow roses.

ACKNOWLEDGMENTS

A writer works alone, putting words on the page, but creating a book is a team effort. It's been a joy to work with a great team to bring this book to you:

Erica Moroz is the talented writer who adapted my adult history book, *The Woman's Hour: The Great Fight to Win the Vote*, into this edition for younger readers. Her translation is faithful, her writing vivid, and she gives a lively spin to this important historical story. My editors at Random House, Sara Sargent and Sasha Henriques, are delightful collaborators, offering their expertise, enthusiasm, and deadline diligence to keep this project on track. Illustrator Debbie Powell captures the story in gorgeous drawings and brings graphic excitement to these pages.

Every creative project begins with an idea, and the

inspiration for transforming *The Woman's Hour* into this book for young readers came from my brilliant literary agents, Dorian Karchmar and Jamie Carr at William Morris Endeavor Agency. Dorian guides my career as agent and enriches my life as friend; and it's been a pleasure to watch Jamie's literary career blossom, and now to partner with her on this project. I also want to thank my wise and witty editor at Viking/Penguin Random House, Wendy Wolf, for making *The Woman's Hour* a book worth reading—and worth adapting into this edition. Just as excellent teachers and coaches push you to work harder to achieve your best, the great editors and agents do the same for their authors.

This book is based upon many months of research and thousands of documents, so I'd like to give a shout-out to the many librarians and archivists, scholars and historians who steered me to the materials I needed. I was able to add depth and detail to the story with the help of descendants and relatives of some of the characters in the story—their family papers and reminiscences were invaluable.

Writing a book takes years—and can feel lonely, all alone at the desk—so I am thankful to my family and friends for cheering me on and sharing this journey with me.

Finally, I've had the pleasure of writing about some of the most amazing women in American history—the suffragists. My heartfelt thanks to them for their skill, courage, and persistence in the struggle.

I hope this story inspires all of you to become activists for a broader and more inclusive democracy. And inspires you—very soon—to vote.

NOTES

CHAPTER 1

4 **"Regard outlook hopeless under present conditions"**: Marjorie Shuler in Nashville to Mrs. Frank Shuler at NAWSA headquarters in New York City, Western Union Telegram, July 10, 1920, Catt Papers, Tennessee State Library and Archives, Nashville.

5 **"The Anti-Suffs will flood Tennessee with the most outrageous literature"**: Carrie Catt to Mrs. John Kenny, June 29, 1920, in Catt Papers, Tennessee State Library and Archives.

8 **"Suffrage Map"**: Versions of the suffrage map were published and displayed by both NAWSA and the Woman's Party and appeared regularly in their publications: NAWSA's *Woman's Journal/Woman Citizen* and the National Woman's Party's *Suffragist*.

9 **"Suffrage supporters feel certain that Tennessee will rise to the occasion"**: "Nation Looks to Solons of State for Ratification," *Nashville Tennessean*, July 18, 1920.

10 **"Our forces are being notified to rally at once"**: Josephine A. Pearson, "My Story: Of How and Why I Became an

Antisuffrage Leader," dated April 30, 1939, Josephine A. Pearson Papers, Tennessee State Library and Archives, microfilm reel #1.

14 **"Lady Warrior":** Biographical details from "Sue Shelton White: Lady Warrior," in *Tennessee Women: Their Lives and Times,* vol. 1, Sarah Wilkerson Freeman and Beverly Greene Bond, eds. (Athens: University of Georgia Press, 2009), 140–63; James P. Louis, "Sue Shelton White and the Woman Suffrage Movement in Tennessee, 1913–1920," *Tennessee Historical Quarterly* 22, no. 2 (1963): 170–90; James P. Louis, "Sue Shelton White," in *Notable American Women: A Biographical Dictionary,* 1607–1950, ed. Edward T. James et al. (Cambridge, MA: Harvard University Press), III: 590–92; Marjorie Spruill Wheeler, *New Women of the New South: The Leaders of the Woman Suffrage Movement in the Southern States* (Oxford and New York: Oxford University Press, 1993). Wheeler, *Votes for Women! The Woman Suffrage Movement in Tennessee, the South, and the Nation* (Knoxville: University of Tennessee Press, 1995), 214–23.

14 **"relentlessly":** White's report to Alice Paul, June 29, 1920, in National Woman's Party Papers, Library of Congress, microfilm reel #79; also in "Suffs Ask for $10,000 for Tennessee Fight," *Baltimore Sun,* July 5, 1920.

CHAPTER 2

21 **His 1916 manifesto:** *An Address to the Men of Tennessee on Female Suffrage,* by John J. Vertrees, pamphlet (Nashville, 1916) in Abby Crawford Milton Papers, Scrapbooks, Tennessee State Library and Archives. Also reprinted in Wheeler, *Votes for Women!,* 197–213.

CHAPTER 4

32 **She recalled that once, as a little girl, in a fit of rage:** Elizabeth Cady Stanton, *Eighty Years and More* (1898) (Boston: Northeastern University Press, 1993).

33 **Declaration of Sentiments:** Elizabeth Cady Stanton, Susan Bronwell Anthony, et al., eds., *History of Woman Suffrage*, vol. 1. (New York: Fowler and Wells, 1881), 53.

34 **"Woman's Rights Man":** Philip S. Foner, ed., *Frederick Douglass on Women's Rights* (Westport and London: Greenwood Press, 1976), 10–15.

35 **"That is just what I wanted":** Elizabeth Stanton to Lucretia Mott, September 30, 1848, in Elizabeth Cady Stanton and Harriot Stanton Blatch, *Elizabeth Cady Stanton as Revealed in Her Letters, Diary and Reminiscences*, II: 20–22.

35 **"I forged the thunderbolts":** Stanton, *Eighty Years*, 165.

36 **"There can never be true peace in this republic":** Descriptions of the work of the Woman's Loyal League can be found in Eleanor Flexner and Ellen Fitzpatrick, *Century of Struggle: The Woman's Rights Movement in the United States* (Cambridge, MA: Belknap Press of Harvard University Press, 1996), 103–6; Venet, 94–122; Faye E. Dudden, *Fighting Chance: The Struggle over Woman Suffrage and Black Suffrage in Reconstruction America* (Oxford and New York: Oxford University Press), 51–57.

CHAPTER 5

45 **"My time, my strength, and my influence":** "Cox Promises to Help," *Chicago Tribune*, July 17, 1920; "Cox Promises Aid to Suffs," *Baltimore Sun*, July 17, 1920.

47 **"return to normalcy":** "Harding Finishes Acceptance Speech," *New York Times*, July 18, 1920.

48 **"The womanhood of America"**: Text of Warren G. Harding's acceptance speech, *New York Times,* July 23, 1920.

48 **"Only by action"**: "Women Displeased by Harding's Stand," *New York Times,* July 23, 1920.

CHAPTER 6

49 **"The very safety of Southern civilization"**: Mrs. James S. Pinckard to Gov. James Cox, July 26, 1920, reprinted in *Woman Patriot* 4, no. 31 (July 31, 1920).

51 **"We are determined to prevent"**: "Antis will fight," *Chattanooga Times,* July 18, 1920.

53 **"sex war"**: Rowe's testimony is in "Extending the Right of Suffrage to Women: Hearings Before the Committee on Woman Suffrage," House of Representatives, Sixty-Fifth Congress, on H. J. Res. 200. January 3–7, 1918, 323.

55 **"What will the Negro woman do"**: Pierce's speech is in *Nashville Tennessean,* May 19, 1920, p. 8; also quoted in Carol Lynn Yellin, Janann Sherman, and Ilene Jones Cornwell, *The Perfect 36: Tennessee Delivers Woman Suffrage* (Memphis: Serviceberry Press, 1998), 71–73; and Anita Shafer Goodstein, "A Rare Alliance: African American and White Women in the Tennessee Elections of 1919 and 1920," *Journal of Southern History* 64, no. 2 (May 1998): 239.

CHAPTER 7

57 **"I have come to help you"**: Catt to Tennessee League of Women Voters, Nashville, July 21, 1920, Catt Papers, Tennessee State Library and Archives.

58 **"That unheard from number":** Catt to Tennessee League of Women Voters, Nashville, July 21, 1920, Catt Papers, Tennessee State Library and Archives.

61 **She didn't beat around the bush:** Details of Catt's speech in "Catt Talks to Kiwanis Club," *Nashville Banner*, July 23, 1920, and in "Catt Defends Ratification Plans," *Nashville Banner*, July 24, 1920.

62 **She and Marjorie Shuler quickly wrote a press release:** Press release, July 25, 1920, Abby Milton Papers, Tennessee State Library and Archives; "Tennessee Safe for Suffrage Says Mrs. Catt," *Nashville Tennessean*, July 26, 1920; "Poll Suffrage Majority," *Washington Post*, July 26, 1920.

62 **That morning the *Banner* had published an attack letter:** *Nashville Banner*, July 25, 1920.

CHAPTER 8

65 **"The President is responsible for the betrayal of American Womanhood":** Description of the protest from Sue Shelton White, "Militant Suffragists and How They Won a Hopeless Cause," written for the *Montgomery (AL) Times*, August 1919, unpublished typescript, White Papers, Schlesinger Library, Harvard University; "The Demonstration of February 9," *Suffragist*, February 22, 1919; Louisine Havemeyer, "Memories of a Militant: The Prison Special," *Scribners*, May 1922; "Suffragists Burn Wilson in Effigy," *New York Times*, February 10, 1919; Stevens, chapter 22.

65 **Louisine, who was a wealthy New York widow:** Louisine Havemeyer, "Memories of a Militant: The Prison Special," *Scribners*, May 1922.

70 **"I unalterably oppose suffrage"** and *Cannot vote for amendment*: "Harding Fails to Change Candler's View," *Chattanooga News,* July 28, 1920, Catt Papers, Tennessee State Library and Archives.

71 *Lady here wants to know:* This telephone call is described in Inez Haynes Irwin, *The Story of Alice Paul and the National Woman's Party* (Fairfax, VA: Denlinger's Publishers, Ltd., 1964), 473. Irwin interviewed Pollitzer and other Woman's Party staff working in Tennessee as soon as they returned to headquarters in Washington.

72 *Harry will be all right:* Pollitzer to Paul, July 29, 1920, National Woman's Party Papers, Library of Congress.

CHAPTER 9

78 **keep your "hands off"**: Letter to the presidential candidates in "Nominees Urged to Leave Suffrage Alone," *Nashville Tennessean,* August 6, 1920. Letter to Tennessee Legislators in "Officers Named to Constitution League," *Nashville Tennessean,* August 4, 1920.

78 **At noon on Wednesday:** "Mrs. Catt Is Luncheon Guest," *Chattanooga News,* August 4, 1920.

CHAPTER 10

84 **"re-open the horrors of Reconstruction":** "Anti-Suffragists to Open Exhibit Here," *Nashville Banner,* n.d. (early August 1920). Anti-ratification literature in Josephine Pearson Papers, Tennessee State Library and Archives.

85 **"Mrs. Catt's Bible":** "Anti-Suffragists to Open Exhibit Here," *Nashville Banner,* n.d. (early August 1920). Anti-ratification

literature in Catt Papers and Josephine Pearson Papers, Tennessee State Library and Archives.

CHAPTER 11

88 **He'd had a "change of conviction":** William's meeting with Seth Walker is described in Carol Lynn Yellin, "Countdown in Tennessee, 1920," *American Heritage* 30 (1978): 12–23, 27–35, 97.

91 **"mysterious influences":** "Mighty Battle Is in Prospect over Suffrage," *Nashville Tennesseean,* August 8, 1920.

CHAPTER 12

94 **"Tennessee occupies a pivotal position":** "Roberts Urges Ratification," *Nashville Banner,* August 9, 1920.

96 **That's when he finally revealed himself:** Irwin, 469. See also "Eyes on Solons," *Memphis News-Scimitar,* August 9, 1920; and "Ratification More Remote," *Chattanooga Times,* August 10, 1920.

97 **Seth was now announcing:** "Ratification Seems More Remote," *Chattanooga Times,* August 11, 1920; "Suffrage Resolution to Go to Committee," *Nashville Tennesseean,* August 11, 1920; "Miss Williams Gets Factions Together," *Memphis News-Scimitar,* August 10, 1920.

98 **"I'd let the old Capitol crumble":** *Knoxville Journal,* August 11, 1920, quoted in a letter from Mary Winsor to Betty Gram Swing, July 6, 1943, in Betty Gram Swing papers, Schlesinger Library, Harvard University. Gram's encounter with Walker is also related in "Outlook Not Encouraging," *Charlotte (NC) Observer,* August 11, 1920; "Speaker Walker to Fight Suffrage Resolution," *Chattanooga Times,* August 11, 1920; and "Suffs

Turning on Democrats in Tennessee," *Baltimore Sun,* August 11, 1920.

99 **"I have absolute confidence":** "Move Made to Block Suffrage Vote," *Memphis News-Scimitar,* August 11, 1920.

100 **"We are not going to be thrust aside":** "Outlook Not Encouraging," *Charlotte (NC) Observer,* August 11, 1920.

101 **"I have become convinced":** "Speaker Walker to Fight: Other Members Join in Opposition," *Chattanooga Times,* August 11, 1920.

CHAPTER 13

102 **As William stood before the chamber:** Accounts in "Defeat Effort to Defer Ratification," *Nashville Banner,* August 11, 1920; "House Beats Motion to Refer Suffrage," *Nashville Tennesseean,* August 12, 1920; "Move Is Made to Block Suffrage Vote by Postponement," *Memphis News-Scimitar,* August 11, 1920; "Effort to Postpone Action on Suffrage," *Chattanooga News,* August 11, 1920; "Postponement Would Mean Procrastination," *Chattanooga News,* August 11, 1920; and "Suffs Win in Tennessee," *Charlotte (NC) Observer,* August 12, 1920.

105 **"The people of Tennessee have already passed"** and **The roll call began:** "Defeat Effort to Defer Ratification," *Nashville Banner,* August 11, 1920.

110 **"The eyes of the United States"** and **"Suffrage leaders are working":** Accounts of the debate are in "Debate Suffrage at Joint Hearing," *Nashville Banner,* August 13, 1920; "Ratification Is Debated Before Packed Audience," *Nashville Tennessean,* August 13, 1920; "Harding Letter Depresses Suffs," *Memphis News-Scimitar,* August 13, 1920; "Gen. Cates Turns Batteries on Traducers of Tennessee Womanhood," *Chattanooga News,*

August 13, 1920; "Candidate Will Not Urge Vote," *Chattanooga Times,* August 13, 1920; and *New York Times,* August 13, 1920.

CHAPTER 14

114 **The committee "is of the opinion"** and ***This federal amendment:*** Accounts of the debate and passage are in "Senate Ratifies Suffrage Amendment," *Memphis News-Scimitar,* August 13, 1920; "Senate Ratifies Suffrage After Fight," *Nashville Tennessean,* August 14, 1920; "State Senate Ratifies," *Chattanooga News;* "Senate Ratifies by Expected Majority," *Nashville Banner,* August 13, 1920; "Senators Bow Under Lash of Bosses," *Chattanooga Times,* August 14, 1920; "Tennessee Senate Ratifies," *New York Times,* August 14, 1920; "Upper House Votes to Ratify," *Charlotte (NC) Observer,* August 14, 1920; and "Candler Hissed by Senators," *Chattanooga News,* August 14, 1920.

116 **"That is the most unfortunate":** "Action Expected on Tuesday," *Harrisburg (PA) Evening News,* August 13, 1920.

CHAPTER 15

119 ***Big deal!:*** "Senate Action Does Not Worry Antis," *Nashville Banner,* August 14, 1920.

121 **"the earnest hope that the house":** "Wilson Wires to Walker for Aid," *Nashville Tennessean,* August 14, 1920.

122 **"I have the profound":** "Can't Vote Contrary to His Conviction," *Chattanooga News,* August 14, 1920; "Tension Relaxes in Suff Battle," *Nashville Tennessean,* August 15, 1920.

122 **"vulgar, ignorant, insane":** Jacqueline Van Voris, *Carrie Chapman Catt: A Public Life* (New York: Feminist Press, 1987), 160; Catt in *Woman Citizen,* September 4, 1920.

124 **"I believe one of the most powerful lobbies":** "Big Interests in Plot," *Charlotte (NC) Observer,* August 16, 1920; "Declare a Strong Lobby Is Working in Tennessee," *Harrisburg (PA) Evening News,* August 16, 1920.

125 **"We now have 35½ states":** Catt to Mary Gray Peck, August 15, 1920, Catt Papers, Library of Congress. Also in Mary Gray Peck, *Carrie Chapman Catt: A Biography* (New York: H. W. Wilson, 1944), 335.

CHAPTER 16

130 **"We've got 'em":** Robert B. Jones and Mark E. Byrnes, "The 'Bitterest Fight': The Tennessee General Assembly and the Nineteenth Amendment," *Tennessee Historical Quarterly* 68, no. 3 (Fall 2009): 275, quoting from *Knoxville Journal and Tribune,* August 17, 1920.

131 **"I have here the pledges":** "House Delays Suffrage Vote Until Today," *Nashville Tennessean,* August 18, 1920.

134 **"I cannot pledge myself":** Irwin, 473–74.

CHAPTER 17

141 **"We really trusted you":** Irwin, 474.

142 **"The hour has come":** Accounts of the vote in "Suffrage Amendment Adopted by House," *Nashville Tennessean,* August 19, 1920; "Tennessee Now Perfect 36," *Chattanooga News,* August 18, 1920; "House Passes Resolution," *Chattanooga Times,* August 19, 1920; "Suffrage Forces Victorious in House," *Nashville Banner,* August 18, 1920; "Tennessee Solons Ratify Suffrage," *Memphis News-Scimitar,* August 18, 1920; "Tennessee Completes Suffrage Victory," *New York Times,* August 19,

1920; "Suffrage Ratification Completed," *New York Tribune,* August 19, 1920; "Tennessee Ratifies," *Washington Post,* August 19, 1920; and "Speaker Walker Changes Vote," *Baltimore Sun,* August 19, 1920.

147 **In his jacket pocket sat the letter:** Letter of Phoebe (Febb) Ensminger Burn to Harry Burn, August 17, 1920, in Calvin M. McClung Historical Collection, Knox County Library, Knoxville, TN.

CHAPTER 18

152 **"Splendid Work. Hold the Fort":** Congratulatory telegrams in National Woman's Party Papers, Library of Congress.

152 **"The civilization of the world"** and **"All along I have wished":** "Ratification Acclaimed by Party Heads," *Nashville Tennessean,* August 18, 1920.

153 **"Our mothers began it":** "Mrs. Catt Tells of Fight," *Baltimore Sun,* August 19, 1920.

153 **"With the power to vote achieved":** "Colby to Proclaim Suffrage Promptly," *New York Times,* August 19, 1920.

155 **"The action of Tennessee":** Franklin D. Roosevelt to A. H. Roberts, Roberts Papers, Tennessee State Library and Archives.

155 **But Albert also received other telegrams:** Men of Fayetville to Gov. A. H. Roberts, August 18, 1920, and W. Lamb to A. H. Roberts, August 18, 1920, in Roberts Papers, Tennessee State Library and Archives; "Resentment in Lincoln County," *Nashville Banner,* August 19, 1920.

157 **"I want to state":** "Proud of Opportunity to Free Women," *Chattanooga News,* August 19, 1920; "Tennessee Delays Fight," *Memphis News-Scimitar,* August 19, 1920; "Charges of Fraud in Suffrage Fight," *New York Times,* August 20, 1920.

160   **"You are all heroes"**: *Nashville Tennessean*, August 21, 1920.

160   **"The victory is complete"**: "Suffs Elated," *Nashville Tennessean*, August 21, 1920.

160   **"tired and heart-sick"**: Pearson, "My Story," and in Wheeler, *Votes for Women!*, 241.

162   **"Woman's Suffrage is now a fact"**: "W. H. A. Moore," *Baltimore Afro-American*, August 27, 1920.

162   **On Friday morning**: Peck, 340–42; "Bringing the Victors Home," *Woman Citizen*, September 4, 1920.

164   **"The vote is the emblem"**: Catt in *Woman Citizen*, September 4, 1920; also in Peck, 342.

CHAPTER 19

166   **"Tell us what you want voted"**: Pearson, "My Story."

169   **"We must not rest"**: Mary White Ovington, "Free Black as Well as White Women," *Suffragist*, November 1920. Also handwritten letter to the editor of the *Suffragist* from Ella Rush Murray, November 15, 1920, NAACP Papers, Library of Congress.

SELECTED BIBLIOGRAPHY

ARCHIVAL COLLECTIONS

Tennessee State Library and Archives, Nashville, TN

Tennessee State Museum, Nashville, TN

Calvin M. McClung Historical Collection, Knoxville Public
Library, Knoxville, TN

University of Tennessee Knoxville Libraries, Special Collections

Albert Gore Research Center, Middle Tennessee University,
Murfreesboro, TN

Schlesinger Library on the History of Women in America,
Radcliffe Institute for Advanced Study, Harvard University,
Cambridge, MA

Library of Congress, Manuscript Division, Washington, D.C.

New York Public Library, Manuscript Division, New York, NY

Historical Society of Pennsylvania, Philadelphia, PA

Pennsylvania State University, Harrisburg, PA, Alice Marshall
Women's History Collection

South Caroliniana Library, University of South Carolina, Columbia, SC

South Carolina Historical Society/College of Charleston Libraries, Charleston, SC

Southern Oral History Program Collection, University of North Carolina, Chapel Hill, NC

Woodrow Wilson Presidential Library, Staunton, VA

Warren G. Harding Home Presidential Site, Marion, OH

National First Ladies' Library, Canton, OH

NEWSPAPERS AND PERIODICALS

Baltimore Sun

Brooklyn Daily Eagle

Charlotte (NC) Observer

Chattanooga News

Chattanooga Times

Christian Science Monitor

Crisis (Journal of the NAACP)

Kingsport (TN) Times

Knoxville Journal

Los Angeles Times

Memphis Commercial Appeal

Memphis News-Scimitar

Nashville Banner

Nashville Tennessean

New York Evening World

New York Herald

New York Times
Suffragist
Washington (D.C.) Herald
Washington Post
Woman Citizen
Woman Patriot
Woman's Journal
Woman's Remonstrance

SELECTED BOOKS

Baker, Jean H. *Sisters: The Lives of America's Suffragists.* New York: Hill and Wang, 2005.

Baker, Jean H., ed. *Votes for Women: The Struggle for Suffrage Revisited.* Oxford and New York: Oxford University Press, 2002.

Benjamin, Anne Myra Goodman. *Women Against Equality: A History of the Anti-Suffrage Movement in the United States from 1895 to 1920.* Lewiston, NY: Edwin Mellen Press, 1991.

Berg, A. Scott. *Wilson.* New York: G. P. Putnam's Sons, 2013.

Camhi, Jane Jerome. *Women Against Women: American Anti-Suffragism, 1880–1920.* Brooklyn, NY: Carlson Publishing, 1994.

Catt, Carrie Chapman, and Nettie Shuler. *Woman Suffrage and Politics: The Inner Story of the Suffrage Movement.* New York: C. Scribner's Sons, 1926.

Cott, Nancy F. *The Grounding of Modern Feminism.* New Haven: Yale University Press, 1987.

Douglass, Frederick, and Philip Sheldon Foner. *Frederick Douglass on Women's Rights*. Westport, CT, and London: Greenwood Press, 1976.

DuBois, Ellen Carol. *Feminism and Suffrage: The Emergence of an Independent Women's Movement in America, 1848–1869*. Ithaca, NY: Cornell University Press, 1999.

——. *Harriot Stanton Blatch and the Winning of Woman Suffrage*. New Haven, CT: Yale University Press, 1999.

Dudden, Faye E. *Fighting Chance: The Struggle over Woman Suffrage and Black Suffrage in Reconstruction America*. Oxford and New York: Oxford University Press, 2011.

Flexner, Eleanor, and Ellen Fitzpatrick. *Century of Struggle: The Woman's Rights Movement in the United States*. Cambridge, MA: Belknap Press of Harvard University Press, 1996.

Fowler, Robert Booth. *Carrie Catt: Feminist Politician*. Boston: Northeastern University Press, 1986.

Franzen, Trisha. *Anna Howard Shaw: The Work of Woman Suffrage*. Champaign: University of Illinois Press, 2014.

Freeman, Sarah Wilkerson, Beverly G. Bond, and Laura Helper-Ferris. *Tennessee Women: Their Lives and Times*. Vol. 1. Athens: University of Georgia Press, 2009.

Giddings, Paula J. *Ida: A Sword Among Lions: Ida B. Wells and the Campaign Against Lynching*. New York: Amistad, 2008.

Ginzberg, Lori D. *Elizabeth Cady Stanton: An American Life*. New York: Macmillan, 2010.

Goodier, Susan. *No Votes for Women: The New York State Anti-Suffrage Movement*. Champaign: University of Illinois Press, 2013.

Gordon, Ann D., ed. *The Trial of Susan B. Anthony*. Washington, D.C.: Federal Judicial Center, 2005.

Green, Elna C. *Southern Strategies: Southern Women and the Woman Suffrage Question.* Chapel Hill: University of North Carolina Press, 1997.

Harper, Ida Husted, ed. *History of Woman Suffrage (1900–1920).* Vol. 6. New York: National American Woman Suffrage Association, 1922.

Harper, Ida Husted. *The Life and Work of Susan B. Anthony.* Indianapolis and Kansas City: Bowen-Merrill, 1898.

Irwin, Inez Haynes. *The Story of Alice Paul and the National Woman's Party.* Fairfax, VA: Denlinger's Publishers, 1964. Originally published 1921.

Jablonsky, Thomas J. *The Home, Heaven, and Mother Party: Female Anti-Suffragists in the United States, 1868–1920.* Brooklyn, NY: Carlson Publishing, 1994.

James, Edward T., Janet Wilson, and Paul S. Boyer, eds. *Notable American Women: A Biographical Dictionary, 1607–1950.* 3 vols. Cambridge, MA: Harvard University Press, 1971.

Keyssar, Alexander. *The Right to Vote: The Contested History of Democracy in the United States.* New York: Basic Books, 2000.

Kraditor, Aileen S. *The Ideas of the Woman Suffrage Movement, 1890–1920.* New York: Columbia University Press, 1965.

Kraft, Barbara S. *The Peace Ship: Henry Ford's Pacifist Adventure in the First World War.* New York: Macmillan/McGraw-Hill, 1978.

Lash, Joseph P. *Eleanor and Franklin.* New York: W. W. Norton, 2014.

Levin, Phyllis Lee. *Edith and Woodrow: The Wilson White House.* New York: Scribner, 2001.

Lindenmeyer, Kriste. *Ordinary Women, Extraordinary Lives: Women in American History.* Lanham, MD: Rowman & Littlefield, 2000.

Lutz, Alma. *Susan B. Anthony: Rebel, Crusader, Humanitarian.* Boston: Beacon Press, 1959.

Marshall, Susan E. *Splintered Sisterhood: Gender and Class in the Campaign Against Woman Suffrage*. Madison: University of Wisconsin Press, 1997.

McMillen, Sally. *Seneca Falls and the Origins of the Women's Rights Movement*. Oxford: Oxford University Press, 2008.

Miller, Kristie. *Ellen and Edith: Woodrow Wilson's First Ladies*. Lawrence: University Press of Kansas, 2015.

Milton, Abby Crawford. *Report of the Tennessee League of Women Voters: Containing a Full Account of the Suffrage Ratification Campaign*. Monograph, 1921.

Naparsteck, Martin. *The Trial of Susan B. Anthony: An Illegal Vote, a Courtroom Conviction and a Step Toward Women's Suffrage*. Jefferson, NC: McFarland, 2014.

National American Woman Suffrage Association. *Victory: How Women Won It: A Centennial Symposium, 1840–1940*. New York: H. W. Wilson, 1940.

Painter, Nell Irvin. *Sojourner Truth: A Life, A Symbol*. New York: W. W. Norton, 1997.

Park, Maud Wood. *Front Door Lobby*. Boston: Beacon Press, 1960.

Peck, Mary Gray. *Carrie Chapman Catt: A Biography*. New York: H. W. Wilson, 1944.

Pietrusza, David. *1920: The Year of the Six Presidents*. New York: Basic Books, 2009.

Roosevelt, Eleanor. *The Autobiography of Eleanor Roosevelt*. Boston: Da Capo Press, 1992.

Scott, Anne Firor. *The Southern Lady: From Pedestal to Politics, 1830–1930*. Charlottesville: University of Virginia Press, 1995.

Showalter, Elaine. *These Modern Women: Autobiographical Essays from the Twenties*. New York: Feminist Press, 1989.

Sklar, Kathryn Kish. *Women's Rights Emerges within the Anti-Slavery Movement, 1830–1870: A Brief History with Documents.* Boston: Bedford/St. Martin's, 2000.

Stanton, Elizabeth Cady. *Eighty Years and More (1898).* Boston: Northeastern University Press, 1993.

Stanton, Elizabeth Cady, and Susan Brownell Anthony. Edited by Ann D. Gordon. *The Selected Papers of Elizabeth Cady Stanton and Susan B. Anthony: Against an Aristocracy of Sex, 1866 to 1873.* New Brunswick, NJ: Rutgers University Press, 2000.

Stanton, Elizabeth Cady, Susan Brownell Anthony, Matilda Joslyn Gage, and Ida Husted Harper, eds. *History of Woman Suffrage (1848–1861).* Vol. 1. Rochester, NY: Susan B. Anthony, 1887.

Stanton, Elizabeth Cady, and Harriot Stanton Blatch. *Elizabeth Cady Stanton as Revealed in Her Letters, Diary and Reminiscences.* New York: Harper & Brothers, 1922.

Stevens, Doris. *Jailed for Freedom: American Women Win the Vote.* New York: Boni and Liveright, 1920. Rev. ed. Edited by Carol O'Hare. Troutdale, OR: New Sage Press, 1995.

Taylor, A. Elizabeth. *The Woman Suffrage Movement in Tennessee.* New York: Bookman Associates, 1957.

Tennessee Historical Society. *Tennessee Encyclopedia of History and Culture* (online edition). Knoxville: University of Tennessee, 2018. tennesseeencyclopedia.net.

Terrell, Mary Church. *A Colored Woman in a White World.* Amherst, NY: Humanity Books, 2005. Originally published 1940.

Tetrault, Lisa. *The Myth of Seneca Falls: Memory and the Women's Suffrage Movement, 1848–1898.* Chapel Hill: University of North Carolina Press, 2014.

Upton, Harriet Taylor. *Random Recollections*. Manuscript. Alice Marshall Collection, Library, Pennsylvania State University, Harrisburg.

Van Voris, Jacqueline. *Carrie Chapman Catt: A Public Life*. New York: Feminist Press, 1987.

Venet, Wendy Hamand. *Neither Ballots Nor Bullets: Women Abolitionists and the Civil War*. Charlottesville: University of Virginia Press, 1991.

Walton, Mary. *A Woman's Crusade: Alice Paul and the Battle for the Ballot*. New York: Macmillan, 2010.

Wellman, Judith. *The Road to Seneca Falls: Elizabeth Cady Stanton and the First Woman's Rights Convention*. Champaign: University of Illinois Press, 2004.

Wells, Ida B. *Crusade for Justice: The Autobiography of Ida B. Wells*. Chicago: University of Chicago Press, 2013.

Wheeler, Marjorie Spruill. *New Women of the New South: The Leaders of the Woman Suffrage Movement in the Southern States*. Oxford and New York: Oxford University Press, 1993.

———. *Votes for Women! The Woman Suffrage Movement in Tennessee, the South, and the Nation*. Knoxville: University of Tennessee Press, 1995.

Wineapple, Brenda. *Ecstatic Nation: Confidence, Crisis, and Compromise, 1848–1877*. New York: HarperCollins, 2013.

Yellin, Carol Lynn, and Janann Sherman. *The Perfect 36: Tennessee Delivers Woman Suffrage*. Memphis: Serviceberry Press, 1998.

Zahniser, J. D., and Amelia R. Fry. *Alice Paul: Claiming Power*. Oxford and New York: Oxford University Press, 2014.

INDEX

ABOUT THE AUTHOR

ELAINE WEISS is a journalist and author whose magazine feature writing has been recognized with prizes from the Society of Professional Journalists, and her byline has appeared in many national publications, as well as in reports for National Public Radio. Elaine's book about the woman's suffrage movement, *The Woman's Hour: The Great Fight to Win the Vote* (Viking/Penguin), has earned glowing reviews from the *New York Times*, the *Wall Street Journal*, and NPR, among others, and she has presented talks about the book and the woman's suffrage movement across the country. Elaine lives in Baltimore, Maryland, with her husband, and they have two grown children. When not working at her desk, she can be found paddling her kayak on the Chesapeake Bay. And she votes in every election.